RESOURCE BOOKS FOR TEACHERS

series editor
ALAN MALEY

CLASSROOM DYNAMICS

Jill Hadfield

Oxford University Press

OXFORD

UNIVERSITY PRESS

Great Clarendon Street, Oxford OX2 6DP

Oxford University Press is a department of the University of Oxford.
It furthers the University's objective of excellence in research, scholarship,
and education by publishing worldwide in

Oxford New York

Auckland Cape Town Dar es Salaam Hong Kong Karachi
Kuala Lumpur Madrid Melbourne Mexico City Nairobi
New Delhi Shanghai Taipei Toronto

With offices in

Argentina Austria Brazil Chile Czech Republic France Greece
Guatemala Hungary Italy Japan Poland Portugal Singapore
South Korea Switzerland Thailand Turkey Ukraine Vietnam

OXFORD and OXFORD ENGLISH are registered trade marks of
Oxford University Press in the UK and in certain other countries

ISBN-13: 978 0 19 437147 6
ISBN-10: 0 19 437147 6

Typeset by Wyvern Typesetting Ltd, Bristol

Printed in China

Acknowledgements

I would like to thank the staff and students of the following institutions who sent replies to the questionnaires 'Moaning and Groaning in the Foreign Language Staffroom' 1 and 2, and 'The Old Lags' Project':

Bell School, Cambridge; Bell School, Norwich; Bell School, Saffron Walden; Bourneville College; Bradford and Ilkley College; Brighton Polytechnic; Cambridgeshire College of Arts and Technology; Centre for Applied Language Studies, Reading; Christchurch College, Canterbury; Eurocentre, Bournemouth; Eurocentre, Forest Hill; Filton Technical College; Greenhill College; Hammersmith and West London College; Kilburn Polytechnic; Kingsway College; The Language Centre of Ireland; Millbank College; Pilgrims, Canterbury; Redbridge Technical College; Tresham College.

Particular thanks are due to: Rod Bolitho, Larry Cole, Charlie Hadfield, Maggy McNorton, Jenny Pearson, Gill Porter-Ladousse, Adrienne Short, Tessa Woodward, and all the staff of the Language Centre, South Devon College of Arts and Technology for stimulating discussions and revealing insights into group problems.

Above all, my thanks go to Angi Malderez, with whom this project began, and who has contributed more than I can possibly acknowledge to my understanding of groups and how they work.

The Publishers and I wish to thank the following for permission to reproduce copyright material. There are instances where we have been unable to trace or contact copyright holders before our printing deadline. We apologize for this apparent negligence, and if notified will be pleased to rectify any errors or omissions at the earliest opportunity.

'A Boy's Head' (p 58) from Miroslav Holub: *Selected Poems* translated by Ian Milner and George Theiner (Penguin Books, 1967), copyright © Miroslav Holub, 1967, Translation copyright © Penguin Books, 1967. First four lines from 'People' (p 85) from Yevtushenko: *Selected Poems* translated by Robin Milner-Gulland and Peter Levi, SJ (Penguin Books, 1962), copyright © Robin Milner-Gulland and Peter Levi, 1962. 'The Door' and 'Tonight at Noon' by Adrian Henri, published by André Deutsch. 'The Twelve Days of Christmas' from *The Oxford Christmas Carol Book* © Oxford University Press, 1988. Melody for 'Five gold rings' added by Frederick Austin, and reproduced by permission of Novello & Co. Ltd. Zodiac chart adapted from *Project Video 3* published by Oxford University Press.

For Angi

Contents

The authors and series editor

Jill Hadfield is a freelance teacher trainer and author who has worked at Bordeaux University in France, at Central China Agricultural University on a World Bank Project run by Bell Educational Trust, at Tibet University on a British Council project, and most recently in Madagascar on a British Council/ODA project where she was responsible for designing materials for and training teacher-trainers, and in the EFL section at South Devon College of Arts and Technology, UK. She is the author of *Presenting New Language* and four Skills books in the Oxford Basics series, as well as *Elementary Communication Games, Intermediate Communication Games, Advanced Communication Games* and *Reading Games*, and the co-author with her husband, Charlie, of *Writing in English 3, Writing Games*, and two travel books: *Watching the Dragon* and *A Winter in Tibet*. She has also published a novel: *Postcards from Babel* (1991).

Alan Maley worked for The British Council from 1962 to 1988, serving as English Language Officer in Yugoslavia, Ghana, Italy, France, and China, and as Regional Representative in South India (Madras). From 1988 to 1993 he was Director-General of the Bell Educational Trust, Cambridge. From 1993 to 1998 he was Senior Fellow in the Department of English Language and Literature of the National University of Singapore. He is currently a freelance consultant and Director of the graduate English programme at Assumption University, Bangkok. He has written *Literature*, in this series, *Beyond Words, Sounds Interesting, Sounds Intriguing, Words, Variations on a Theme*, and *Drama Techniques in Language Learning* (all with Alan Duff), *The Mind's Eye* (with Françoise Grellet and Alan Duff), *Learning to Listen* and *Poem into Poem* (with Sandra Moulding), and *Short and Sweet*, and *The English Teacher's Voice*. He is also Series Editor for the Oxford Supplementary Skills series.

Foreword

This book tackles that most elusive, yet crucial, of factors in classrooms—the 'atmosphere'. Why does one group 'gel' while another gives off 'bad vibes'? We all know that if the atmosphere, the 'feel' is right, learning is facilitated.

As the author says, 'a positive group atmosphere can have a beneficial effect on the morale, motivation, and self-image of its members, and thus significantly affect their learning, by developing in them a positive attitude to the language being learned, to the learning process, and to themselves as learners' (page 10).

But can something so intangible and insubstantial as an 'atmosphere' be created? This book is an attempt to show that it can.

The author begins by analysing what characterizes successful and unsuccessful groups. She goes on to offer a range of activities to develop such positive characteristics as mutual trust, confidence in self and in the group, empathy within the group, and the building of a group identity.

Many teachers will be familiar with 'warmers' and other activities designed to facilitate group formation. The originality of this book lies in its attention to the group process throughout the lifetime of the group. By far the majority of the activities are designed to sustain the life of the group after it is up and running. There are also suggestions for preparing students for the end of the group experience to avoid the sometimes painful withdrawal symptoms which follow the disbanding of a tightly-knit learning community.

The activities and comments are always practicable and are clearly based on the author's long and varied experience (from Torquay to Tibet!). She makes no great theoretical claims but the whole book is infused with two rare qualities—common sense, and good-humoured kindness. Teachers at all levels will find it invaluable.

Alan Maley

A boy's head

In it there is a space-ship
and a project
for doing away with piano lessons.

And there is
Noah's ark,
which shall be first.

And there is
an entirely new bird,
an entirely new hare,
an entirely new bumble-bee.

There is a river
that flows upwards.

There is a multiplication table.

There is anti-matter.

And it just cannot be trimmed.

I believe
that only what cannot be trimmed
is a head.

There is much promise
in the circumstance
that so many people have heads.

Miroslav Holub

Introduction

I didn't mean to write this book.

I actually set out with a colleague, Angi Malderez, to write a completely different book, on learner training. But before beginning, we decided to do a little fact-finding and try to discover a bit more about the problems involved in the learning process, as perceived by both teachers and learners. To this end, we sent out two questionnaires to language schools and state colleges all over Britain. The first, called 'Moaning and Groaning in the Foreign Language Staffroom', invited teachers to list their most common staffroom moans about problems involved in the teaching/learning process: the kind of preoccupation that fills your head when you have just finished a lesson you were not completely satisfied with. The second, called 'The Old Lags' Project', asked teachers to invite their outgoing students at the end of a term to write a letter to an imaginary new student, explaining the difficulties they had found in learning English, and offering advice.

The replies to 'Moaning and Groaning' took us by surprise. Teachers nationwide seem to be far less worried by such concerns as finding new and exciting ways to teach the present perfect or getting students to retain new vocabulary items, than by the atmosphere in the class and the chemistry of the group. By far the most common complaint was, as one teacher put it, 'My group just doesn't gel!' There were many variations on this theme, for example:

- The same students always answer questions, quieter members can't get a word in.
- No-one can understand what X says and the others laugh at him. Y is more serious then the others and is getting frustrated. Z has been here two terms and has seen it all. He's bored.
- A refuses to work with anyone.
- Students are very bad at listening to each other.
- I have a 'spirit-killing' student who is bored with everything.
- I have a split-level class with language ghettos.
- Disappointing lack of interest in talking to each other and learning about other cultures.
- B wants to study grammar and the others don't so he brings up grammar at the end of every lesson and then always doubts my explanations. The others get irritated by this.
- Student 'passengers' make no contribution to the group.

- C is only interested in hearing herself speak and seems jealous if the teacher's attention is drawn to anyone else.
- They're only concerned with what they want out of the lesson and show no feeling for their peers.
- They're a really odd mixture.
- I can't establish a co-operative feeling.

At a workshop for teachers following this survey, we asked teachers what it felt like to have a group that 'did not gel'. They discussed their experiences and brainstormed a list of symptoms of 'lack of gel'. They produced the following list:

- Students don't listen to each other.
- They don't laugh at each others' jokes.
- They don't make jokes.
- They can't deal with problems: molehills become mountains.
- They stay in nationality groups.
- They are territorial; they don't like regrouping.
- They are culturally intolerant.
- They don't socialize outside the classroom.
- They are all sitting in silence when you go in.
- They make you dread teaching.
- They won't work with each other.
- Nothing you do seems to work and the harder you try, the worse it gets.
- The more uncooperative they are, the worse you teach, the more uncooperative they are, and so on.
- There is often an 'indigestible' group member.
- They question everything you do and if you make a mistake they crucify you.
- They are teacher-dependent.
- They all want different things and won't compromise.
- There is no trust.

This showed that all the teachers present recognized the problem and knew exactly what it felt like. The teachers at the workshop were all very experienced and included teacher-trainers, heads of departments, materials writers, and EFL experts of various kinds, which shows that the problem is not confined to inexperienced and trainee teachers.

The 'Old Lags' Project' was, disappointingly, far less revealing, mostly, I think, because it was mistaken in concept: students at the end of their stay in Britain are not in a particularly analytical frame of mind. We should really have asked for comments from the sticky middle of a term. But many replies indicated that group dynamics were an important concern for students too, with such comments as:

'In this term I found good friends and a kind teacher so I progressed a lot.'
'Learning English is a love and heat (sic) relationship.'

'I like the people and also the English language. It can make you suffer but it's beautiful.'
'I do prefer to work in groups, couples, but the classroom mates (*sic*) not everyone is friendly.'
'The students are very young. I think you could feel quite strange in these groups.'
'I am blessed with good teacher and good friends in class.'
'The teacher is a friend more. He will help you. You will find several difficulties but you will never feel sad or angry.'

These comments showed that the affective side of language learning is very important to students.

So I turned my attention from learner training and began to think hard about groups in general, and my own experience of them in particular. In common with the teachers who wrote the cries of despair on the questionnaire, my own most miserable teaching experiences have been due not to the inadequacy of any particular textbook, or lack of proper classroom facilities, but to a negative atmosphere that somehow built up in the group. In fact, the worst moments of my teaching career were in the company of a group of affluent, well-educated, sophisticated Europeans, in a well-equipped and well-resourced EFL department in the UK, using an enjoyable and lively textbook; whereas one of the most rewarding teaching experiences I have had was teaching TOEFL, not the most inspiring of material, from dog-eared, badly stencilled copies, to a group of Tibetans in an unheated room without electricity in the middle of a Tibetan winter ($-20°C$).

The factor that transformed what should have been an EFL paradise into a month-long nightmare, and what should have been an EFL nightmare into a delightful and rewarding experience was the indefinable one of group chemistry. What *was* the difference? Was it simply that the students in the second group were nicer people than those in the first? Or was it that the Tibetans, less sophisticated and worldly than their European counterparts, were content with less? Or were they more used to living in a group, co-operating with and supporting each other, than Europeans, brought up to fight for their individuality? Or was it that the Tibetans liked each other, whereas the Europeans did not? Or did I teach one group well and the other badly? Or did I unconsciously do some things that increased antagonism, or even led to it, with the members of the first group, and other things that increased solidarity and co-operation between members of the second group?

The difference was probably due to a combination of some or all of these factors, but whereas we can do very little about the first four, it is possible to modify the last two. Bad teaching may be transformed into better teaching with the aid of the many teacher-training materials and resource books for teachers that already exist. However, it seems to me that very little material exists to offer suggestions for practical things a teacher can do to improve relations and atmosphere within a group. Whereas a lot of attention has been paid to the way we form groups and the initial stage of group life, very little attention has been paid to the process of maintaining groups after they have been formed. Teacher-training materials offer guidance on the selection of techniques appropriate to a particular teaching point, but less thought has been given to their possible effect on the group dynamic.

But why should we pay attention to group processes? Isn't our job simply to teach efficiently? Surely the group process can look after itself? The way the students in the class relate to each other is not the teacher's business; the teacher's business is to transmit content, and whether the class get on with each other or not is irrelevant. However, that is not the message I got from the cries of misery from staffrooms all over Britain, and I am convinced that a successful group dynamic is a vital element in the teaching/learning process.

Firstly, and most obviously, teaching and learning can and should be a joyful experience for both teacher and learner, and most teachers, except the very lucky or the very talented, will know from bitter experience that there is no more miserable teaching experience than to be shut up inside the four walls of your classroom with a prickly and uncooperative group.

Secondly, whereas in the days of rote-learning and teacher-dominated classrooms the relationship between teacher and group was paramount and the question of interrelationships within the group was not vital, in present-day EFL classrooms, where pairwork and groupwork have become the norm, relationships within the group become more important: it is fundamental to the success of these activities to have support and co-operation from the group and a harmonious relationship between its members. Where students act as a pool of resources for each other, refusal to co-operate means that a vital element of the learning process is missing. A group whose members are not on speaking terms will not learn much in a student-centred classroom!

Finally, and perhaps most importantly, research in social psychology confirms what teachers know instinctively: a cohesive group works more efficiently and productively (see Michael Argyle 1969, *The Social Psychology of Work*). A positive group atmosphere can have a beneficial effect on the morale, motivation, and self-image of its members, and thus significantly affect their learning, by developing in them a positive attitude to the language being learned, to the learning process, and to themselves as learners.

Successful groups can thus be, as T. Douglas puts it in *Groups—Understanding People Together* (1983), 'an instrument of behavioural or attitudinal change, an instrument of support and maintenance, a pool of resources, and an instrument to facilitate learning'. To that I would like to add they can also be a lot of fun.

But what is a successful group? The teachers whose comments on their unhappy experiences with groups are given at the beginning of the introduction, seemed fairly clear about the characteristics of an *unsuccessful* group, so perhaps that is a good place to start. To rephrase their comments in more general terms, an unsuccessful group in language learning terms is one where:

- The individuals in the class do not cohere into a group.
- There is an uncomfortable, tense, or negative atmosphere.
- The members of the group are all intent on their individual ambitions and are unwilling to compromise or define group goals for learning.
- Some members of the group will not participate in group activities.
- Some members of the group tend to dominate group activities at the expense of shyer members.
- The members of the group are territorial or cliquey and will not interact equally with all members of the group.
- Members of the group will not listen to one another.
- Group members are not interested in each other and are even antagonistic towards each other.
- Group members are not self-reliant but dependent on the teacher.
- Group members cannot put problems in perspective; trivial things develop into major upsets.
- There may be an 'indigestible' group member who causes problems or creates a negative atmosphere.
- Group members will not co-operate to perform tasks.
- Members of the group do not trust each other.
- Individuals in the group are competitive and attention-seeking.
- Members of the group are intolerant of cultural and personal differences.
- Group members have certain fixed or rigid ideas which they are reluctant to modify.
- Members of the group lack responsibility: they are reluctant to make an effort or take the initiative.
- Group members tend to be over-serious with little sense of fun.
- Group members lack confidence in themselves as learners, what they are learning, and the way they are being taught.

In contrast, a successful group, I suggest, will be one where:

- The group is cohesive, and members have a definite sense of themselves as a group.
- There is a positive, supportive atmosphere: members have a positive self-image which is reinforced by the group, so that they feel secure enough to express their individuality.
- The members of the group are able to compromise. They have a sense of direction as a group and are able to define their goals in group, as well as individual, terms.
- Group members are not cliquey or territorial but interact happily with all members of the group.
- Members of the group listen to each other, and take turns.
- Group members are interested in each other and feel they have something in common.
- The group is self-reliant and has a sense of responsibility. It is able to overcome problems and difficulties without recourse to the teacher.
- The group is tolerant of all its members; members feel secure and accepted.
- Members co-operate in the performing of tasks and are able to work together productively.
- The members of the group trust each other.
- Individuals in the group are not competitive and do not seek individual attention at the expense of others.
- Group members are able to empathize with each other and understand each others' points of view even if they do not share them.
- Group members are open-minded, flexible, and receptive to new ideas.
- The group has a sense of fun.
- Group members have a positive attitude to themselves as learners, to the language and culture being studied, and to the learning experience.

How is it that some groups develop into the latter kind of group, while some groups develop into the former? Is there anything we as teachers can do to encourage development of the positive characteristics of the second group and discourage the negative qualities of the first?

In this book I examine the characteristics of a successful group, and suggest practical ways in which the teacher can develop a cohesive and supportive group atmosphere of a kind conducive to learning. I approach this by re-examining traditional classroom activities from the point of view of their effect on group dynamics, and by suggesting new activities which may promote a successful group dynamic. I also try to provide a framework for integrating these activities into a teaching syllabus. Before going on to make these suggestions, however, I have a few caveats and reservations:

1 I am not suggesting that the only purpose of an EFL class is to have a good time with your group and that a group experience can replace content teaching. On the contrary, if you do this you will sabotage the group atmosphere very quickly: students realize when they are not learning and nothing destroys a group atmosphere more than the feeling of not learning anything. However, I am suggesting that it can be a good idea when selecting from a range of techniques available for a particular teaching point to be aware of their possible effect on group dynamics as well as their appropriacy for the teaching point, and even occasionally to plan in activities that may be unrelated to the syllabus but which have a positive effect on group cohesion.

2 I am not suggesting that groups should be forced into a particular mould or made to conform to a type, though I am suggesting that it is better to have a positive rather than a negative atmosphere. The activities in this book should provide a framework for individuals in the class to come together and establish their own group identity, which will be different for every group. The delight of teaching is the different, spontaneous, and very individual ways in which groups will respond to activities.

3 Some people may feel that the very act of thinking about group dynamics and how we can affect them suggests manipulation. However, as teachers, we are, whether we like it or not, manipulators of people. Whatever we do, or do not do, in the classroom will have its effect, positive or negative, on the dynamics of the group. Since we are in such a responsible position, I think it only fair that we should be aware of our actions and the possible effects they might be having, and should choose to do those things which are more likely to have a positive effect on the individuals we are dealing with.

4 This book is not a piece of academic research, offering solid conclusions based on statistical proof; it is much more intuitive, exploratory, and tentative than that. Several sources have fed into the ideas in the book. Some ideas do derive from other people's academic research, such as work by social psychologists on the functioning of the group; some derive from my own *ad hoc* explorations into teachers' problems with groups, and some from my own varied experiences of what it feels like to be a language learner. But most ideas in the book come from a mixture of my own experiences as a classroom teacher, my colleagues' experiences and ideas on groups, and my own intuition, together with a determination to look at classroom practice from a different angle.

5 Lastly, I am not proposing this book as a universal panacea for all group problems. As outlined above, there are many factors which determine the dynamics of a group. I do believe that most groups have the potential to become supportive, cohesive, and co-operative, given the right conditions and enough encouragement, but group dynamics is ultimately a matter of chemistry, and there is not much even the most dedicated teacher can do with a group of determinedly prickly individuals (except perhaps to forget the concept of a group and individualize their learning as far as possible!) Conversely, there are plenty of teachers who teach very successfully and have happy, well-motivated classes without using any of the techniques in this book. This book is not intended to convert, nor is it intended as a formula. It is just an attempt to look at a problem which concerns us all and to come up with some practical suggestions which teachers can select and adapt according to their own needs and preferences and those of their group. I hope, of course, that teachers will find these useful, but group dynamics is above all a matter of the personality and style of the teacher, the personalities of the people in the group, and the complex interrelationships between them, and it is up to the individual teacher to establish a relationship with the students in his or her own distinctive way. There is a limit beyond which the mere textbook writer cannot and should not presume to interfere!

How to use this book

How the book is organized

The book is divided into three sections, dealing with the processes of forming, maintaining, and ending groups respectively. The first and last sections are both short, containing activities suitable for the first and last weeks of a course. The bulk of the book, in the central section, explores what can be done to maintain a good group atmosphere over a term, or a year.

In each section there are both affective and cognitive activities. The affective activities aim to create a positive and supportive group atmosphere in a non-explicit way; the cognitive activities seek to make certain demands of the group learning process more explicit to the learner. Obviously, some aspects of group life must be encouraged in an affective way; for example, it would be difficult to create a climate of trust simply by convincing students intellectually that it is important to trust the other members of the group. However, other aspects, such as defining goals, demand explicit treatment: knowing where you are going and what you want to achieve is an intellectual matter rather than an emotional one. Personally, I feel both are important, but certain groups and certain teachers may have a preference for one over the other.

Section A, on the affective side, presents activities necessary to break the ice, to introduce group members to each other, and to create a relaxed and supportive atmosphere. On the cognitive side it aims to raise learner awareness of what learning in a group involves, and to give the group a sense of direction by encouraging them to define their goals.

Section B, the central, most important, section, takes the various characteristics of a successful group as outlined in the Introduction and suggests practical classroom techniques the teacher can use to encourage these characteristics. For example, Chapter 4, 'Bridging gaps', suggests activities which will increase the students' awareness of what they have in common and help to bridge personal and cultural differences. Chapter 5, 'Maintaining fluidity', suggests techniques to encourage students to interact with different group members and discourage 'cliqueyness'. Chapter 6, 'Getting to know each other', deals with activities that encourage the students to exchange personal information, and Chapter 7, 'I did it your way', takes this a step further by introducing activities that encourage students to see things from another's point of view.

Activities in Chapters 4–13 are all affective in that they are not overt or explicit in intent, but generally have a language focus; the effect on the group dynamic is a by-product. The remainder of the activities in this section are cognitive, seeking to make some aspects of group processes clearer to the students, and helping them to understand what they are doing, where they are going, and why. Chapter 16, 'A sense of direction', for example, deals with goal defining, assessing, and resetting, and Chapter 17, 'Coexistence and compromise', deals with the need to compromise in order to achieve group goals. Chapter 18, 'Coping with crisis', shows some typical ways in which things can go wrong. It gives examples and case studies of different types of problem, and suggests techniques for resolving them. I have tried to offer some comfort by showing that even if not every problem can be solved, at least you are not alone!

Section C, 'Ending the group experience', suggests activities that round off the group experience in such a way that group members do not feel abandoned, but have a chance to reflect on it and its meaning for them. They can then look forward in order to define their future language learning goals once the group life is over.

Who this book is for

This book was written mainly in response to feedback from a questionnaire sent to language schools and colleges, and so largely reflects the concerns of language school rather than secondary school teachers. In some ways the two are faced with rather different problems of group dynamics: the language school teacher is faced with problems stemming from small, claustrophobic groups, where the individuals are in close contact for sometimes up to thirty or thirty-five hours a week, often made up of adults who come to the course with adult problems and complexes and often very fixed ideas of what they want and what they expect to get. In Britain there may also be the additional problem of reaction to a foreign, alien culture. The secondary school teacher, on the other hand, faces group dynamics problems of discipline, large classes, and motivation. These seem to me to be a very different issue, and one that falls outside the scope of this book. I hope, however, that where there is an overlap between the two sets of problems, for example where there is a need to build a feeling of group solidarity and co-operation, that secondary school teachers will find some of the activities useful. For this reason, I have tried to ensure that many activities have a linguistic aim as well as a group dynamics aim, and that most require little in the way of additional materials or preparation time.

How to use the activities

Since this book is rather different from most resource books of ELT activities, in certain ways it is necessary to explain how I see the activities being used.

Firstly, it is not a course book and not all the activities will be suitable for every group. Activities from the book may be slotted into coursework or used in addition to a textbook as the teacher sees fit; it is up to the individual teacher to select activities that he or she feels happy to use and considers appropriate for his or her particular group at a particular point in time.

However, it differs from a 'dip in, fish out, and slot in' type of resource book since the activities are rather more interdependent. The book tries to offer an integrated approach to the dynamics of the group, and one activity from the book used in isolation or out of context will probably not have a significant or lasting effect on group atmosphere. The topics treated in the book are all different facets of the same process, the development of a cohesive and supportive group. Each activity is part of a process which needs careful thinking out in advance by the teacher and careful maintenance as the course progresses. It is not appropriate to include one activity from Chapter 10, 'Staying positive', for example, without thinking carefully about how you are going to try and maintain a positive atmosphere over the term, and it is not workable to focus on this one topic while neglecting others such as building co-operation and empathy. Using the book necessitates an integrated and balanced approach.

Moreover, this book is not an emergency handbook! The chapter on 'Coping with crisis' does aim to offer support and help to the teacher facing difficulties with a group, but the bulk of the activities in the book are designed to establish and maintain a cohesive, supportive group atmosphere from the beginning of the group's life together; they are not designed to repair things that have gone badly wrong. If your group has somehow developed into a negative, ungenerous, antagonistic collection of individuals, then I would be very cautious about using some of the activities in the book, particularly some of the more affective ones, though you may well have more success with some of the cognitive activities which are designed to get students thinking about aspects of working together. On the other hand, you might consider that if nothing you have tried so far is working, then you might as well see if a new approach works. In this case you would need to think very carefully both about an overall strategy—why you are doing this and what you want to achieve by it—and about individual responses to the activities. What will you do in the case of a frosty reception, refusal to co-operate, or even hostility? Can you turn it to the group's advantage or will it cause the situation to deteriorate even more?

I think, then, that the book needs to be read right through first and the issues in it thought about both in general and in relation to your own teaching and your own groups, before any specific activity is used with a group. It will probably help most to read this book at the end of a term, after an experience, successful or unsuccessful, with a group, and to use it to help you re-examine what you are doing, consciously or unconsciously, with groups. Are you neglecting anything? Are you overdoing anything? Are there any aspects of group life you feel you haven't thought about enough? Are there any activities you think you could usefully include to encourage a more supportive and cohesive group atmosphere? Every group is different, and the balance and emphasis of activities will need to be different for every group you teach. In the end it is a matter of your temperament, your class's temperament, the complex interaction between them, and ultimately your own sensitivity, that must determine how you structure group activities, what you include, and what you leave out.

Selecting and integrating activities

Several considerations will ultimately determine how you select activities and integrate them into your teaching:

- your personality and teaching style
- the composition of your group
- the rhythm of the lesson, the week, and the term
- the constraints of your syllabus.

1 Teaching style

Some teachers may feel more comfortable with certain activities than with others. There may even be some you cannot imagine yourself using at all! Obviously you must select in the first instance activities that you feel comfortable using. If you feel constrained or awkward, then your group is not likely to feel at ease either. On the other hand, an open mind and willingness to experiment may give you some pleasant surprises!

2 Composition of the group

The nature of the individuals making up your group will be one of the main factors in determining which activities you select. An intellectual group may appreciate and respond better to the more cognitive activities such as those in Chapter 16, as may students with a very rigid, traditional educational background. Such students, in whom the force of tradition is very strong, as well as those from a very different cultural background, may respond less well to the more affective activities, though paradoxically you may well feel that such affective activities are exactly what the group needs most! In this case you will have to introduce them gradually, perhaps with some rationale, to convince students intellectually, or emphasize strongly the language learning aspect of such activities. On the other hand, I have had many groups of such students who responded very enthusiastically to the affective activities, in reaction against their background, and who tended to spurn the more cognitive activities. With such a group, or a group that has become 'high' on group atmosphere, you may have to redress the balance by including more cognitive activities to try to establish more sense of direction and prevent the group from becoming an emotional swamp. A very disparate group, composed of many different personalities, nationalities, or ages, may benefit most from the gap-bridging activities in Chapter 4, the empathy activities in Chapter 17, and the group-building activities in Chapters 8, 11, and 13. With a group composed of distinct factions (for example, two nationality blocs) it will also be essential to keep seating arrangements fluid, using techniques from Chapter 5. A shy group will need some of the exercises from Chapter 14 to encourage participation, and may also benefit from the trust activities in Chapter 7 and, if they have a tendency to self-doubt and negativity, from exercises such as those in Chapter 10 which encourage positive feelings. A group where there are several dominant, self-willed, or intolerant individuals may benefit from the activities in Chapters 17 and 7, which encourage them to appreciate other points of view and to seek compromise. They will undoubtedly also benefit from the activities in 'Learning to listen' (Chapter 15) and can be given more sense of group solidarity with others in the group via activities in Chapters 4 and 8.

Whatever the composition of your group, you will probably find that the dynamics shift during the course of a term and what was an appropriate strategy in the first weeks may no longer be suitable or necessary by mid-term. When planning out what activities to select, you will need to be constantly responsive to changes in roles and relationships within the group.

3 Warming up, cooling down, taking a break: rhythms of a lesson, a week, a term

Learning a new language is an intense experience, requiring a lot of concentration. There will inevitably be times when students lack energy, feel pressurized, or have reached saturation point; when they need warming up, cooling down, or a break in the rhythm.

When students come into their first lesson in the morning their energy level will be low. They may be half-awake, their minds may be full of last night's problems or a row they had at breakfast, they may not have spoken English since you last saw them. It is important to begin the morning with a short, not-too-demanding activity which will energize people and put them in the mood for learning and also incidentally allow time for latecomers to arrive before you start the lesson. Some of the short activities in Chapters 9, 'Establishing trust', and 10, 'Staying positive', could be used here, and the reseating games in Chapter 5 are a good way to get students moving around and talking to each other at the beginning of a lesson.

At the end of a lesson, and particularly at the end of a morning or afternoon, some time needs to be spent on the opposite process: cooling down. Lessons can often end very abruptly with the teacher realizing that there isn't time for everything on the lesson plan, breaking off an activity as the bell rings, and hurriedly setting homework. If two or three lessons end like this in the same morning, the effect on the students can be to make them feel harried and under pressure. It is important to give students time to reflect on what they have done and what they have learned during the day. The activity 'Have I got what I wanted?' in Chapter 16, for example, will encourage students to summarize lesson content and to see its relevance to themselves.

In the middle of a morning or afternoon, half-way through a double lesson, or after a difficult activity or one requiring a lot of concentration, it is important to give students a break. Students may also welcome this as a short respite from the group: a short individual breathing space. I think it is important that such breaks should be non-verbal—a brief holiday from words. You could try the relaxation exercise in 16.2, 'Visualize it', for example, or play some quiet music and ask the students to listen to it with eyes closed for a few minutes.

A week and a term will have their own rhythms too, similar to those of a lesson or a day. Monday morning is notorious, and if you can spare the time, it is worth devoting the first lesson on a Monday to a positive, group-forming, energizing activity, such as those in 'Bridging gaps' (4), 'Staying positive (10), or 'A sense of belonging' (8), before going on to talk about aims for the week ahead. The end of the week, like the end of a lesson, is a time for cooling down, for taking stock of what has been achieved in the week, and clarifying goals for the next week. A mid-week break can be a good idea too, in the shape of a lesson or even a whole morning that is different from the others. You might put two classes together and team-teach, or perhaps devote some time to project work, video, creative writing, or drama. Some of the shorter activities in 'Group achievements' (11) would be suitable here.

The format of this book itself echoes the rhythm of a term, with the first section containing warm-up activities for the first days of the group's life together, and the final section devoted to cooling-down activities to round off the group experience in the last days of term. The middle of a term is often a period where students experience a slump. They may become bored with routine, or depressed because they feel they are not absorbing new language any more or working as well as they did at the beginning. If you do not have a half-term break, the middle of term is a good place for a few days or even a week of completely different activity. Some of the longer activities in Chapter 11, such as a mini-project, a magazine, or a video programme, would both provide a break in routine and give the group a sense of solidarity and achievement—something they badly need if they are going through a mid-term slump.

4 Integrating activities into the syllabus

If you have a tightly packed programme, or a rigid syllabus, or are teaching towards an examination, you may be wondering how you can afford the apparent luxury of group dynamics exercises. However, the majority of the activities in the book have a dual function, and differ only from other language practice activities in that they have an affective purpose tucked inside the language learning purpose. Most of the activities, therefore, will not need a special 'group dynamics' slot on the timetable, and can form part of the normal language syllabus as grammar, speaking, or writing practice. The only difference will be that considerations of group dynamics should form part of your criteria for selecting these activities. For example, if you need a writing activity that practises the simple past, but want at the same time to increase group solidarity, you would do better to choose an activity like 'Rainy Sunday Shock Horror' (8.3), or 'Group history' (8.1) rather than a gap-fill exercise or essay on 'What I did last weekend' set for homework. Similarly, an exercise like 'Changing places' (5.2) will fulfil the triple function of quickly revising a structure taught the previous day, warming students up, and keeping seating arrangements fluid to discourage the formation of cliques. Two 'Language focus indexes' are provided at the back of the book to enable easy cross-reference between affective and linguistic aims.

While it should not be necessary for you to make a distinction for the students between these activities and other language practice activities, there are some activities in the book whose purpose will need to be made explicit, since they are cognitive rather than affective, that is, their purpose is to encourage the students to think about and understand some element of the learning process. These activities, in Chapters 14, 15, 16, and 17, will need to be built into the course in some way. The compromise and negotiation activities in Chapter 17 will need some time (two to three lessons) allotted near the beginning of a term, when you are deciding on course content. The initial activities on defining and setting goals in Chapter 16 will also need some time (one to two lessons) allotted at the beginning of term, as well as a regular short session each week (15–20 minutes) for assessing and resetting goals. The activities in Chapters 14 and 15, for instance, will need to be programmed into a speaking skills course; they are designed to be used with whatever materials form the basis of your course. The feedback techniques in Chapter 12 should also form a regular part of a speaking skills course. Another regular feature you should build into the course if possible is a 'warm-up' slot at the beginning of a morning (see 3 above). All of these features of the course, unlike those with a self-evident language practice aim, will need to be explained to the students with a brief rationale, such as 'I'd like to start each morning with a short "warm-up" activity, just to make you feel relaxed and get you in the mood for thinking in English'.

Section A
Forming the group

Introduction

I have always liked this poem:

> Go and open the door.
>   Maybe outside there's
>   a tree, or a wood,
>   a garden,
>   or a magic city.
>
> Go and open the door.
>   Maybe a dog's rummaging.
>   Maybe you'll see a face,
> or an eye,
> or the picture
>   of a picture.
>
> Go and open the door.
>   If there's a fog
>   It will clear.
>
> Go and open the door.
>   Even if there's only
>   the darkness ticking,
>   even if there's only
>   the hollow wind,
>   even if
>   nothing
>   is there,
> go and open the door.
>
> At least
> there'll be
> a draught.

Miroslav Holub

To open the classroom door on the first morning of term and go in to face a completely new class is to open the door on the unknown. Behind that closed door a whole termful of laughter, jokes, discoveries, warmth, co-operation, and friendship could be waiting for you. Alternatively, there could be a whole termful of friction, disagreements, hostile silences, and frustration. Even after fifteen years of teaching, I can never open that door without a mixture of anticipation and trepidation.

It is obviously important to begin to establish a good group atmosphere right from the first lesson. The students in the group may be strangers to each other; they may also be nervous, worried, lacking in confidence, unsure of their capabilities, and wondering what they have let themselves in for. In forming the group, therefore, it is important to relax the students and relieve the tension they may be feeling, to introduce them to each other, and to encourage them to begin to get to know each other. But it is also important to begin to help the students to become aware of what is involved both in learning a language and working together in a group, to begin to develop both a sense of direction and a feeling of co-operation. The affective and cognitive activities in this section are designed to achieve these aims.

1 Breaking the ice: warm-up activities for the first week of term

Enough has been written about ice-breakers for most teachers to be familiar with the concept and to have their own favourites. Nevertheless, I include some new ones here, together with a few old favourites, in an order in which they could be used in the first week of term to encourage students gradually to reveal more about themselves and find out more about the other group members. The first four activities could be used in the first lesson and the remaining three as warm-up activities to begin each of the subsequent days of the first week.

The main reasons for using ice-breaking activities with a new group are:

1 to get the students to make their initial contacts with each other through English (it is then easier to go on speaking English with each other)

2 to get the students to make contact with as many other people as possible

3 to learn names

4 to find out something about other group members and to begin to get to know them in an informal and friendly way

5 to encourage fluid seating arrangements and discourage 'territoriality'

6 to create a relaxed and enjoyable atmosphere.

1.1 Guess my name

LEVEL
Elementary and above

TIME
5–10 minutes

MATERIALS
One small piece of paper for everyone in the group

PROCEDURE
1 Give a small piece of paper to everyone in the group and ask them to write their first name on it, then to fold it up without showing it to anyone, and to give it to you.

2 Ask the students to sit in a circle and redistribute the names, so that everyone gets a piece of paper with someone else's name on it.

3 Ask everyone to unfold their papers and to look around at the other people in the group and try and guess who the name belongs to. Give them a minute or so to do this silently.

4 Then ask the first student to read out the name on their piece of paper and to say who they think it belongs to, giving a reason if possible, for example, 'I think this man is called Carlos because he has dark hair and looks Spanish'.

5 Then ask the real Carlos to identify himself. Continue in this way until all names have been guessed.

REMARKS

This game can obviously only be played if the students have not yet had a chance to hear each others' names. It is a way of fixing the students' names more firmly in each others' minds than if they merely told each other their names. It is also more fun.

1.2 Shaking hands

LEVEL

All

TIME

5 minutes

PROCEDURE

1 Get all the students walking round the room.

2 Ask them to shake hands with everyone they meet. Ask them to do this formally, though without saying anything, as if at an official occasion. Demonstrate.

3 As they and you continue walking and shaking hands, ask them to say their name, again formally. Demonstrate.

4 As you all continue walking round and shaking hands, ask them to present the person they have just shaken hands with to someone else, again formally: 'Let me introduce you to . . .', 'This is . . .', 'Pleased to meet you'.

5 Ask them to continue meeting, shaking hands, saying their name, and presenting people they have just met to someone else.

VARIATION

When this has gone on a little while and you think they probably know two or three names, stop them and tell them that this time they are walking down a street where they keep seeing old friends. They should wave at their friend, yell their name, and rush up and greet them. Demonstrate this yourself with one student.

1.3 Circles

LEVEL	**Elementary and above**
TIME	**15 minutes**
PROCEDURE	1 Get everyone to stand in a circle facing each other in pairs.

2 Tell them they have two minutes to find out as much as possible about their partner. They can ask anything they like.

3 When the time is up, ask them to turn so that they are back to back with their first partner, facing a new partner. They should now tell their new partner everything they can remember about their first partner.

4 Finally, get them to sit down in the circle and ask them to say anything they know about anyone else in the circle.

1.4 My home town

LEVEL	**Elementary and above**
TIME	**10–15 minutes**
MATERIALS	**Small piece of paper for each student**
PROCEDURE	1 Give out the pieces of paper and ask each student to write three sentences about their home town, but not to mention the name of the town or the country.

2 Collect in the pieces of paper and redistribute them so that each student has a piece of paper describing someone else's home town.

3 Tell the students that they have to find out who lives in the town described on their piece of paper, by asking three questions. Give them a little time to work out the questions if necessary.

4 Then ask the students to get up and mill around freely asking questions until they find the inhabitant of the town described on their paper. They should also find out the name of the town and the country.

5 When they have finished, ask them to stand in a circle and ask each student to say a few words about someone else's home town, for example, 'Ahmed comes from a village in the mountains in Morocco where most people are farmers'.

REMARKS	If you have a class who all come from the same town you can ask them to write about the street or area where they live.

1.5 Group skills

LEVEL	**Elementary and above**
TIME	**10–15 minutes**
MATERIALS	**Questionnaire**
PREPARATION	Set essay two days before and prepare questionnaire on the basis of the information you receive in the essays.
PROCEDURE	1 Ask students to write a short essay about themselves for homework, describing their town, family, hobbies, talents, previous jobs, etc.

PROCEDURE

1 Ask students to write a short essay about themselves for homework, describing their town, family, hobbies, talents, previous jobs, etc.

2 Collect these in and prepare a questionnaire about students' talents and skills using information in the essays (see example below). Make sure you include everyone on the questionnaire.

3 Make enough copies of the questionnaire for everyone in the class.

4 Give out the questionnaires and ask the students to find out who the people are and write their names in the gaps provided.

5 Go through the answers when most people have finished.

SAMPLE QUESTIONNAIRE

> 1 This person would be useful if your car breaks down.
> ....
>
> 2. Ask this person for help if you have a mathematical problem.
> ....
>
> 3 If you want something translated into Russian, ask this person. ....
>
> 4 Ask this person to bring his guitar to class sometime and we'll learn some English songs. ....

1.6 Family statistics

LEVEL	**Lower-intermediate and above**
TIME	**10–15 minutes**
MATERIALS	**Copy or copies of the questionnaire**
PREPARATION	Copy and cut up the questionnaires so that each student has one question to answer.

PROCEDURE

1 Give out the questions and ask the students to complete them, by going round and asking questions to collect the necessary information.

2 When everyone has finished, sit them in a circle and ask them to share the results of their research. If you wish you can ask them to make a poster displaying the information.

QUESTIONNAIRE

Who comes from the largest family?	How many people think they resemble their father most?
How many people are the eldest in the family?	How many people had a bossy elder sister?
How many people are the youngest in the family?	How many people have the same job as their father or their mother?
How many people are the middle child?	How many people live with their parents?
How many people are only children?	How many people are married?
How many people think they resemble their mother most?	How many nephews and nieces do the group have in total?
Ask everyone who is the person they are closest to in their family (apart from their parents). Keep a note of the answers and work out which relative most people feel closest to.	Ask everyone who they admire most in their family. Keep a note of the answers and work out some 'statistics': how many people admire their mother most, how many people admire their brother, and so on.

1.7 Forfeits

LEVEL	**Elementary and above**
TIME	**15–20 minutes**
MATERIALS	**One set of forfeit cards** (see below)
PREPARATION	Copy the cards and cut them up.
PROCEDURE	**1** Ask the group to sit in a circle and place one set of cards face down in a pile on a chair in the middle.

2 Nominate one student to begin. Invite this student to ask another student to guess something about them, such as 'Rosanna, can you guess my brother's job?'

3 If Rosanna guesses correctly, the first student must pick up a forfeit card and answer it. If Rosanna cannot guess, she must pick up the forfeit card and answer it.

4 Continue in this way, going round the circle until everyone has had a turn. Make a rule that no one can be asked a question twice.

FORFEIT CARDS

Tell everyone three things about your family.	Tell everyone three things about your home town.
Tell everyone something about your job or school.	Tell everyone about what you did last year.
Tell everyone about the best holiday you ever had.	Tell everyone about the best film you ever saw.
Tell everyone about your hobbies.	Tell everyone three things you like and three things you dislike.
Tell everyone the best book you ever read.	Tell everyone what you like doing at the weekend.

Tell everyone the name of someone you admire, and why.	Tell everyone about a sport you play or watch.
Tell everyone something you would like to be able to do.	Tell everyone about something you can do well.
Tell everyone something about your favourite filmstar or pop singer.	Tell everyone about a dream or an ambition you have.
Tell everyone what makes you happy.	Tell everyone what you would do if you had a free year, and enough money to do whatever you wanted.
Tell everyone about something that is important to you.	Tell everyone where you would like to live best, and why.

Sources and acknowledgements
Activities 2 and 3 are 'old favourites' and will be familiar to many teachers. I first learned them from colleagues at South Devon College and at the Université de Bordeaux III.

2 Thinking about language: individual learning styles and group strategies

Any group of students, brought together for the first time, will have different expectations of what learning a language involves and what they want out of the course. One problem may be that they have not really defined these expectations to themselves; another problem may be that they have never really questioned received attitudes to language learning; yet another problem may be that they are unaware of alternative attitudes to language learning and learning styles. All these problems have the potential to cause friction even in an otherwise good-natured group. Some members of the group may want to study grammar rules, while others think that the way to learn English is by listening and speaking, and forgetting about boring old grammar. Some people are intuitive language learners while others are analytic language learners. Again, some learners are visual types, whereas in others auditory memory is more developed. If each category thinks that its style is the only way to learn, then you have potential for resentment and conflict, unless you help learners to understand how aims, attitudes, and learning styles may differ, and also encourage them to start thinking about how they as a group can reconcile what may be conflicting aims and interests. The activities in this chapter aim to make a start on this process. Obviously, the question of defining goals and learning to compromise to achieve them is a not a simple one or one that can be dealt with in a single lesson. The business of setting, assessing, and resetting goals and of making group decisions and compromises is a continuous process, and further ideas on the subject are to be found in Section B, for example Chapters 16 and 17.

The questionnaires in this chapter aim to help the students become aware of different attitudes to learning and different styles within the group. See also 16.1, 'I'm here because . . .', for a similar questionnaire.

2.1 What kind of person are you?

LEVEL Post-elementary and above

TIME 30 minutes

MATERIALS **Copy of the questionnaire for each student** (see below)

PROCEDURE 1 Give out the questionnaire 'What kind of person are you?' and ask students to complete it individually.

2 When they have completed it, ask them to discuss it with a partner, giving their reasons for choosing each category.

3 Then collect comments from the group on what characteristics belong to each category. Can they make any generalizations?

QUESTIONNAIRE

WHAT KIND OF PERSON ARE YOU?

Are you a tea person or a coffee person?

Are you a morning person or an evening person?

Are you an earth person or a fire person?

Are you a mountain person or a valley person?

Are you a jungle person or a city person?

Are you an indoor person or an outdoor person?

Are you a garden person or a forest person?

Are you a diary person or a knotted handkerchief person?

Are you a straight line person or a loops and curves person?

Are you a sight person or a sound person?

REMARKS 1 The aim of the exercise is to get students thinking about the ways personal styles, tastes, and preferences are related to character, and are not rational but emotional. There may be a variety of theories and generalizations advanced in the group discussion stage. I don't think there are any right and wrong answers, although I have tried, in designing the questionnaire, to highlight some differences that may affect learning styles: sight/sound, rational/emotional, left brain/right brain, tidy/muddly, organized/disorganized, rule-oriented/spontaneous.

2 This activity is designed to prepare students for the following questionnaires.

2.2 What kind of language learner are you?

LEVEL

Post-elementary and above

TIME

30 minutes

MATERIALS

Copy of the questionnaire for each student (see below)

PROCEDURE

1 Give out copies of the questionnaire and ask students to complete it individually. Emphasize that there are no right or wrong answers, but the answers will depend on individual taste and personality.

2 When they have finished, ask them to share their answers with a partner, discussing any differences and the reasons for them.

3 Then bring the activity into a class discussion by asking each student to explain how their *partner* feels about language learning.

4 Open out the discussion into a consideration of differences in approach and learning style, the reasons for these, their relation to personal differences of temperament and character, and the need to accommodate all these differences in the group programme.

REMARKS

1 I like to take in the completed questionnaires at the end of the discussion and to use these as a basis to build up a group profile. Then I write a letter to the group or an individual letter to each student, discussing what they have written on the questionnaire, outlining various things we could do in the lessons together, and inviting replies. It can help to give each student an individual interview sometime in the first week too.

2 Obviously, a lot of the success of this activity depends on how you handle the discussion at the end. Since every group and every teacher is different, this is very much a matter for individual sensitivity, but here are some general guidelines:

– the general aim of the activity is to sensitize students to each others' different needs and preferences, and increase awareness of different approaches to learning, not to reject any learning styles and attitudes as inappropriate in order to impose a uniform approach on the group.

– The students should go away from the discussion aware of the existence of different views and styles in the group and aware of the need to compromise, but confident that you are thinking about them as individuals, and will be doing your best to integrate their different wants and needs into a coherent programme. They should not on any account leave the class feeling depressed about the conflict of opinions and preparing themselves for a fight to get what they want!

QUESTIONNAIRE

WHAT KIND OF LANGUAGE LEARNER ARE YOU?

1 Tick the *three* activities you think are most similar to language learning, and say why.
Do you think learning a language is like:

learning to ride a bike ☐   learning mathematical formulae ☐

learning to play the piano ☐   learning to swim ☐

learning to play chess ☐   learning dates for a history exam ☐

learning to walk ☐   learning to play cards ☐

learning words in a play ☐

2 Try to number the sentences in order:
1=most useful way for me   12=least useful way for me

Which do you think are the best ways to learn English?

learning lists of vocabulary by heart ☐

writing down the translation of every new word or phrase ☐

learning grammar rules, with example sentences ☐

reading as much as possible in class ☐

speaking as much as possible in class ☐

writing everything down in a notebook and learning it ☐

forgetting about grammar and listening to people talking instead ☐

doing lots of grammar exercises—written? ☐

—oral? ☐

getting the teacher to correct you every time you say a sentence ☐

trying to think in English and not translate into your own language ☐

writing essays and getting them corrected by the teacher ☐

     (continued over)

3 What aspects of language do you feel you need most help or practice with?
  Number them in order: 1=need to practice most   7=need to practise least

grammar   ☐   listening   ☐   writing   ☐

vocabulary   ☐   speaking   ☐   pronunciation   ☐

reading   ☐

4 How do you think the following people can help you best?

your teacher   the other people in the group   yourself
your family   people in the street, in shops, etc.

2.3 Experience and expectations

LEVEL

Lower-intermediate and above

TIME

20 minutes

MATERIALS

One copy of the questionnaire for each student

PREPARATION

Make one copy of the questionnaire for each student in the group.

PROCEDURE

1 Give out the questionnaires and ask students to complete them, putting a tick by the sentences that correspond to their previous language learning experience.

2 When they have finished, ask them to discuss their previous language learning experience with a partner. Take a quick census by asking people to raise hands.

3 Then ask them to look at the questionnaire again and to place a cross by the sentences that they expect will be true of the course they are about to follow.

4 Ask them to discuss the results with a partner: are the two sets of answers more or less the same, or very different?

5 Open the discussion out to involve the whole group.

REMARKS

This questionnaire will give you a chance to find out about students' previous language learning experience, and the expectations they have of the course, which may be very valuable if you have students from a very different culture. It will also give you a chance to explain to them something about the kinds of things you or other teachers hope to do on the course and to give them some kind of rationale for activities that they find unfamiliar or strange. If you collect in the completed questionnaires at the end of the session, it will help you build up a profile of the group.

QUESTIONNAIRE

LEARNING A LANGUAGE: EXPERIENCE AND EXPECTATIONS

Think about your previous experience of learning a language. Tick (√) the sentences that are true for you:

1 Learning a language

involves hard work ☐	is painful ☐	is easy ☐
is interesting ☐	is confusing ☐	comes naturally ☐
is difficult ☐	is boring ☐	requires a lot of memorization ☐
is frustrating ☐	can be a lot of fun ☐	

2 When I am speaking a foreign language I:

feel shy ☐	feel confident ☐	feel embarrassed ☐
feel frustrated ☐	feel challenged ☐	feel tongue-tied ☐
feel stupid ☐	feel happy ☐	feel as if I am a different person ☐

3 Learning a language in class involves:

reading a passage and answering questions ☐		frequent tests ☐
translating a passage ☐		role play, mime, and drama ☐
reading literature ☐		following a textbook ☐
writing grammar exercises ☐		making a newspaper ☐
doing a project ☐		letter writing ☐
learning about British culture ☐		practising speaking in pairs or groups ☐
learning grammar rules ☐		listening to a tape and answering questions ☐
dictation ☐		games ☐
listening to the teacher ☐		repeating in chorus ☐
acting a play or a dialogue ☐		practising pronunciation ☐
memorizing passages ☐		class discussion and debates ☐
making a TV or radio programme ☐		songs ☐
reading aloud ☐		writing stories or essays ☐
learning lists of vocabulary ☐		

Now go back to the beginning of the questionnaire. Mark with a cross (✗) the sentences that you expect will be true of the language course you are about to follow.

---

3 Thinking about groups: group strengths, individual contributions

Some frustrations in groups can arise because individuals focus only on the drawbacks of group life and fail to appreciate the benefits. If a student cannot see beyond the temporary frustration of an individual ambition—the class is engaged in a speaking activity when he or she wants to study grammar, for example—to the wider advantages offered by the group, such as support, encouragement, interaction, and opportunity for language practice, then he or she is not likely to be a very co-operative group member. Sometimes just one such student can sour a whole group.

The first questionnaire in this section acts as an introduction to the activities in Chapter 17, 'Coexistence and compromise'. It aims to sensitize students to what living in a group entails, its pressures as well as its rewards, by drawing on the students' experience of previous groups they have been a part of. It also encourages awareness of the need to contribute and to compromise. The other two questionnaires encourage students to think about how members of a group can co-operate, and show specific rules they can apply to ensure that a discussion works successfully.

3.1 Thinking about groups

LEVEL

Post-elementary and above

TIME

One lesson

MATERIALS

Copy of the questionnaire for each student if required

PROCEDURE

1 Give out the questionnaire and get students to work through it individually or in pairs, a section at a time.

2 At the end of each section draw ideas from the whole group and write them on the board. Get students to discuss their answers in pairs.

3 Students then pool ideas as a group, referring to the notes on the board.

4 Go on to the next section and repeat stages 1–3.

VARIATION

Do not give out the questionnaire at all, but pose the questions one at a time to the group and get them to write down ideas individually before opening up the discussion.

REMARKS

Either way, I think it is important to set the activity in stages with time for reflection and discussion, instead of asking students to fill in the whole questionnaire at once.

QUESTIONNAIRE

THINKING ABOUT GROUPS

1 In your life up to now, what groups have you been a member of? (For example, family, church, colleagues at work.) Try to list all the groups.

2 Did you have a good, a bad, or a mixed experience as a member of these groups?

3 Think about the good groups. Did they have anything in common? What do you think these groups *gave* you?

4 What did you give back?

5 What did you have to give up? (Not the same question as 4!)

6 Think about the group you are in now. What do you think they will be able to give you? What can you offer to them? What might you have to give up?

3.2 Contributing to a group

LEVEL

Lower-intermediate and above

TIME

30–40 minutes

MATERIALS

Two group discussion tasks of an appropriate level for your students (from the textbook you are using or a speaking skills resource book, e.g. *Pairwork, Discussions that Work, Conversation*—see 'Further reading' for suggestions); **copy of each questionnaire for each student**

PREPARATION

Copy questionnaires and prepare discussion materials if necessary.

PROCEDURE

1 Divide the students into small groups of four to six and give them the first discussion task.

2 When each group has completed the task, give each member the first questionnaire. Ask them to think about the questions. Emphasize that it is a personal questionnaire and at this stage they should only think about their own answers to the questions, not anyone else's.

3 When they have had a chance to think and answer the questions, give the group the second discussion task.

4 Finally, give out the second questionnaire and ask them to discuss the questions in their group.

QUESTIONNAIRE 1

CONTRIBUTING TO A GROUP

Did you enjoy the discussion? _____ .

Did you contribute any ideas? _____ .

Did you encourage anyone else to contribute ideas? _____ .

Did you remain silent? _____ .

Did you interrupt anyone, or shout them down? _____ .

Is there any way *you* could help the discussion to go better?

– by contributing more? _____ .

– by making a suggestion for organizing the group? _____

    _____ .

– by not interrupting? _____ .

– by listening more carefully to others? _____ .

– by encouraging others to contribute? _____ .

Try to choose *one* way you could help in the second discussion. _____

_____ .

QUESTIONNAIRE 2

CONTRIBUTING TO A GROUP

Which discussion took longer? _____ .

Which was more enjoyable? _____ .

Did more people contribute to the first or the second discussion? _____

_____ .

Did you feel happier or more relaxed about making contributions to the second

discussion? _____ .

Was your contribution welcomed by others? _____

_____ .

Do you feel that people listened better to each other in the first or the second

discussion? _____ .

Is there anything more you could do *as a group* to make discussions successful and

enjoyable? _____

_____ .

3.3 Roles in groups

LEVEL

Intermediate and above

TIME

One lesson

MATERIALS

Two discussion tasks suitable for the level of your group (either from your textbook or a speaking skills resource book); copy of each questionnaire for each student

PREPARATION

Prepare discussion materials as necessary and copy the questionnaires.

PROCEDURE

1 Divide the students into groups of six to eight. Appoint one observer for each group. Tell the class that these will sit a little apart from the group and act as 'group secretary', making notes on what is said in the discussion.

2 Then call the 'secretaries' up to the front as a group and give each a copy of the first questionnaire and ask them to fill it in by placing a tick in the appropriate column each time a member of the group does one of the things mentioned on the questionnaire. There is no need to specify which member of the group did those things.

QUESTIONNAIRE 1

ROLES IN GROUPS

Put ticks (√) in the end column to show how many times each action was performed.

Action	Number of times
Organized the other members of the group	
Contributed an idea	
Encouraged others to say something	
Tried to get everyone to come to an agreement	
Summarized what other people had said	
Evaluated other people's ideas	
Asked people to explain what they meant	
Made everyone laugh	
Tried to smooth out problems	
Was rude about other people's ideas	
Distracted the group by talking about something else	
Interrupted other people to state my own ideas	
Did something else while everyone was talking	
Didn't listen to other people's ideas	
Didn't talk in English	
For observers only: Number of people who did not speak at all	

3 Ask them to return to their groups and give each group its first discussion task. The 'secretary' should play no part in the discussion but fill in the questionnaire while they talk.

4 When they have finished the discussion, give each member of the group a copy of the questionnaire and ask them to try and remember exactly how they contributed to the discussion, and to place a tick in the appropriate column to record how many times

they performed each action. Ask them to reflect (privately) on their role in the group and decide if they need to change it in any way.

5 Ask the observers to show their completed questionnaire to the group.

6 Give out the second questionnaire to each group and ask them to discuss the questions on it.

QUESTIONNAIRE 2

EVALUATE YOUR GROUP PERFORMANCE!

1 Where are most of the ticks? If they are all in the top half of the questionnaire, then you can congratulate yourselves: you are a generally helpful and co-operative group! Well done! If there are some ticks in the bottom half, then you need to think carefully about how you can co-operate better as a group and be more considerate of the feelings of each member of the group. If all your ticks are in the bottom half, well...! Perhaps you had better ask yourself if you really want to learn English!

2 Are there any gaps? For example, have you got enough encouragers in your group? Have you got a peacemaker—someone who tries to smooth over problems and difficulties? Do enough people contribute ideas? Try and see where your *deficiencies* are as a group.

3 Are there too many people doing something? For example, are there too many organizers? A group really only needs one! And if there are too many contributors and not enough summarizers, then your discussions will have plenty of ideas, but no direction! Try and see what are your *excesses* as a group.

4 Make three lists:
  a) Things we should stop doing
  b) Things we should do more of
  c) Things we should do less of
Decide individually what *you* can do to help the group work more smoothly, and to make group discussions more successful and enjoyable for yourselves.

Now try the second discussion!

---

7 When they have finished, give them the second discussion task.

REMARKS

1 The role of observer/scribe is a good one for a domineering or normally voluble student to experience.

2 Obviously, students will not be in the same discussion group for the rest of the term, and therefore the decisions they made about this particular group will not necessarily be valid next time

they have a discussion. However, the process should have given them some general insights into what kinds of group behaviour make a discussion successful, and some particular insights into the kind of role they can play to help a group work more smoothly, which should be helpful to them whatever group they next find themselves in. Perhaps this point is worth making at the end of the lesson.

Section B
Maintaining the group

Introduction

Forming a group is relatively easy: the initial stage of group life
is usually harmonious as students get to know each other and
begin to work together. Maintaining a cohesive group over a
term or a year is far more difficult.

This part of the book deals with activities which help to sustain a
healthy group: establishing trust, maintaining a positive
atmosphere, bridging cultural and personality gaps, maintaining
contact between all members of the group, encouraging students
to participate fully and to listen to each other, developing the
ability to compromise and co-operate, encouraging empathy,
giving the group a clear sense of direction and a sense of
achievement, and developing a sense of cohesion and group
solidarity. It should again be stressed that all these elements are
interdependent: you cannot neglect one without doing damage to
the others, and the teacher, like a juggler, must try to keep all
these concerns in motion at once.

4 Bridging gaps: opinion- and value-bridging activities

One of the richest sources of discussion activities in recent EFL methodology has been the exploitation of the 'gap', whether information gap, opinion gap, or values gap. Questionnaires, ranking activities, and values clarification tasks are all designed to highlight the differences between people and thus to stimulate discussion and debate. In terms of their potential for language exploitation, these are obviously very valuable classroom activities, but from the point of view of successful group dynamics, the effect of a series of such activities over a term or a year, with the consequent constant emphasis on individual differences of opinion or taste, may be to intensify divisions in the group. Groups are more likely to be cohesive and amicable if their members have some things in common. In this section I suggest a counterbalance to this stress on disagreement and individual idiosyncracies, in the shape of some activities I have christened 'bridging' activities, since they are designed to do the opposite to 'gap' activities: namely, to bring people together, by emphasizing the qualities they share rather than what is different about them. I am not, of course, suggesting that such activities should supplant 'gap' activities, nor that conformity of all members to a group norm is a classroom ideal. Individual differences are what make us human! I am merely suggesting that the inclusion of these activities from time to time may have a beneficial effect on classroom dynamics, particularly if your class has recently had a rich diet of opinion gap discussions and heated debates, or if your class is composed of forceful individuals or idiosyncratic personalities!

4.1 One world

LEVEL **Lower-intermediate and above**

TIME **20 minutes to one whole lesson** (depending on how much time you want to devote to the activity)

PROCEDURE **1** Clear a large space in the centre of the classroom.

2 Tell the students that this represents a map of the world (or their country if you have a monolingual group). Tell them which direction is north, then move to take up an appropriate position on the 'map', depending on the country (or town) you come from: for example, if you are English, stand near the 'top' of the 'map' in the middle; if you are Brazilian, stand in the bottom left-hand section.

3 Ask the students to situate themselves in their 'countries' (towns) on the map, using you as an orientation point.

4 Ask everyone in turn to say which country they are. (This gives students with a hazy grasp of geography the opportunity to re-orientate themselves.)

5 Nominate half the students as 'travellers'; the rest are 'hosts'. You can give them 'tickets' if you like.

6 At a signal from you the travellers are to travel to another country they would like to visit. Two travellers cannot visit one host at the same time. When they get there they should try to find as many things as possible that are *the same* in their own country and in the 'host' country: for example, the weather, what people like to drink, main products manufactured, what time people get up, or what people do at the weekends.

7 At a second signal from you, travellers go on to another country and repeat the process.

8 You can repeat this as many times as you like, though if it is to be a prolonged activity, it may be a good idea for travellers and hosts to change roles half-way. If you like, you can make the activity into a game, by announcing that the winners will be the pair who find the largest number of similarities between their countries.

REMARKS **1** If you cannot move the furniture in your classroom, you can still do the activity by asking half the students to remain seated and the other half to travel round. You may have to compromise on the accuracy of your 'map', but the activity will still work.

2 This is an activity for mixed nationality groups, though it could also work with monolingual groups if the students come from different towns or tribes.

4.2 The Flat Earth Society

LEVEL	**Lower-intermediate and above**
TIME	**20 minutes**
MATERIALS	**Pen and paper for each group**
PROCEDURE	**1** Divide the students into groups of six to eight.

2 Give them a time-limit, say 10 minutes, to write down as many statements as possible with which they *all* agree: for example 'The Earth is flat' or 'Politics is a waste of time' or 'Women are more intelligent than men'.

3 At the end of the allotted time ask each group to read out their list. The group with the longest list wins.

4.3 What's so special about us?

LEVEL	**Lower-intermediate and above**
TIME	**10 minutes**

PREPARATION

You will need to know some personal details about the students in your class: for example, the number of people in their families, their ages, likes and dislikes, shoe sizes, and so on. Use this knowledge (secretly) to arrange them into groups, where the members all share a common characteristic, for example, they all come from families of four people, or they all like bananas. Write yourself a list of the members of each group.

PROCEDURE

1 Divide the students into the groups you have decided on, but do not tell them why they have been assigned to those particular groups.

2 When they have assembled in their groups, tell them that the people in their group all have something in common. They have to find out what it is by sharing information about themselves.

3 When they think they have found out what it is that makes them special, they can verify their answer with you.

REMARKS

This makes a good warm-up activity and is a useful way of dividing the students into groups ready for another (longer) activity.

4.4 Elemental passions

LEVEL   **Intermediate and above**

TIME   **One lesson**

PROCEDURE   **1** Ask the students to stand up and move around the class until they find all the other people in the class with the same zodiac sign as they have. (If students are not sure which sign they belong to they should ask you. A chart is provided below for reference.)

2 Ask them to get into four groups: Air, Fire, Earth, and Water, according to which sign belongs to which element (see chart).

3 Ask them to brainstorm a list of the qualities and characteristics that they associate with their element: for example, warmth, passion, quick temper, or brilliance for fire; solidity, practicality, dependability, and so on for Earth.

4 Then ask them to find as many of these qualities as possible that are shared by all members of the group.

ZODIAC CHART

4.5 Happy families

LEVEL

Intermediate and above

TIME

20–30 minutes

PROCEDURE

1 Ask the students to group themselves in different areas of the classroom according to their position in the family: for example, eldest children at the back, middle children on the left, youngest children on the right, only children at the front.

2 Ask them to discuss with the others in their group what it felt like to be in that position in the family, and what effect it had on them. Are there any characteristics they share as only/eldest/youngest/middle children?

4.6 The Smelly-foot Tribe

LEVEL

Elementary and above

TIME

20 minutes to one lesson (depending on number of groups)

PROCEDURE

1 Divide the class into two, three, or four groups, depending on the size of your class.

2 Ask each group to decide on a tribal name for themselves, according to a characteristic they all share: for example, 'The Big Nose Tribe', if they all have big noses, or 'The Opera Buffs', if they all like opera, or 'The Smelly-foot Tribe' if . . .

3 When they have all decided, the other group or groups must guess what they are called. They can ask up to 20 questions, such as: 'Is it something to do with your appearance?' 'Is it because you all like pop music?' The tribe whose name is being guessed may only say 'Yes' or 'No'.

4 When the others have found the principle behind the name, they may have five guesses at the name. This time the tribe may be a little more helpful, telling them if they are nearly right, if any words in the title are right, and so on. Go on until everyone's name has been guessed.

VARIATIONS

If you prefer you can get the whole class to choose a name for itself. Go out of the room while they are doing it and then come back when they are ready and try to guess the name, following the rules above. Or you can make this an inter-class activity, where each class tries to guess the other's name.

4.7 Predicting similarities

LEVEL

Lower-intermediate and above

TIME

15–20 minutes

MATERIALS

One completion sheet for each student (see below)

PROCEDURE

1 Seat students in pairs, back to back if possible, so that they cannot see what their partner is writing.

2 Give out the sentence completion sheets and ask students to write as many entries as possible under each heading, either from their knowledge of the other student, or from what they imagine or guess to be true. Set a time-limit.

3 When the time is up, ask them to turn to face each other and compare lists.

EXAMPLE

COMPLETION SHEET

We are both . . .

We both have . . .

We both like . . .

When we were younger we both used to . . .

In the future both of us will probably . . .

---

5 Maintaining fluidity: reseating and mêlée games

One symptom of lack of cohesion in a group is 'territoriality'. Group members show a marked preference for 'their' seats, and they are reluctant to move to sit with other people. (This is not confined to classrooms—I have also been in staffrooms where this was the case!) Cliques may develop where members are selective about who they work with, sometimes actively refusing to work with certain students. This does not make for a very pleasant classroom atmosphere, and makes the process of organizing discussions and speaking activities fraught with hazards. But good classroom atmosphere is not the only reason for discouraging territoriality. It is important to ensure that students do not always work with the same partner or partners for several reasons: always working with the same partner will place limits on the amount of language used—pairs may develop their own 'restricted code', always using the same vocabulary and phrases. They may also get to know each other too well, and have too few information gaps, thus becoming bored with each other.

Two techniques are suggested here to help alleviate this problem, or, better, to circumvent it before group members begin to get territorial. A group that has already become fiercely territorial will probably make its resentment felt every time you try to get them to change partners.

The first technique, reseating games, is a useful way of reallocating seats to students in a way that is fun and apparently random (though you can rig it in advance if you like). Students will sometimes resent, or wonder why, they are being asked by the teacher to 'Change places' or 'Go and sit next to X', and may feel like a parcel, being moved from place to place at the teacher's whim. Reseating games are a more indirect and tactful way of reorganizing students into groups or pairs.

The second technique, mêlée games, is a good way of ensuring that students talk to everyone else in the room. Because a goal is intrinsic to the game, students have their own purpose in talking to people, and thus do not feel that they are being coerced into talking to someone they do not really want to communicate with.

5.1 Seating plan

LEVEL **All**

TIME **5–10 minutes**

MATERIALS **Master copy of seating plan prepared in advance; cards** (see below)

PREPARATION Make yourself a seating plan of how you would like your students to sit in tomorrow's lesson. For example:

ALICIA   JUAN   SUSANNA   KURT   MONIKA   ABDUL   NORIKO   HANNA

MARION   PAUL

MAGDA   SVEN

Then write cards for each student with an explanation of where they will be sitting. For example:

HANNA

You are sitting facing the blackboard with a dark-haired girl on your right and a tall man on your left.

Remember to write the cards from the point of view of the direction the student will be facing, not from yours at the front of the class.

PROCEDURE 1 This game works best if you are in the room before the students come in, and hand out the cards as they arrive.

2 The students read their cards and find their place for the lesson.

VARIATION

1 Ask students to give themselves a 'title' describing their habits or something about themselves, such as 'Class Clown' or 'Don Juan'.

2 Ask them to write their title down on a piece of paper and give it to you, but not to tell anyone else what it is.

3 Then make cards as above but based on the titles students have chosen for themselves.

EXAMPLE

CLASSROOM ROMEO

You are sitting between THE BOOKWORM
on your right and THE DISCO KING on
your left.

REMARKS

This is a very useful technique which can be adapted to any level, and used to practise many language points: for example, likes and dislikes, hobbies, 'have got', directions, abilities, personality, or opinions. I often use it to revise something learned the day before.

5.2 Changing places

LEVEL

All

TIME

3 minutes

PREPARATION

Prepare small pieces of paper with instructions on them for half the students in the class (a different instruction for each). For example:

Find someone older than you and sit next to them.

Find someone with more brothers and sisters than you and sit next to them.

Find someone who can ride a bicycle and sit next to them.

The instructions should be either very general, as in the above examples, or very specific, based on your knowledge of the students, to enable the 'searchers' to find specific people. (In this case, you will have to work out in advance exactly who you want to sit next to whom, and who is going to be finding and who is going to be found.)

PROCEDURE

1 Ask alternate students to stand up. The rest should remain seated, so that there is an empty seat next to every seated student.

2 Give out the instruction slips to the students who are standing and ask them to find the person described on the slip. To do this, they will have to move around asking the seated students questions, until they find the person who answers the description on the card.

REMARKS

This activity is useful when students have been working with one partner for some time, and you want them to change partners for the next exercise. Again, it can be adapted to any level, and used to practise a wide variety of language items. It will be most successful when the language it practises is related to the language you are in the middle of teaching. For example, if you are teaching 'can', all the instructions should begin 'Find someone who can...'; if you are teaching the past simple, all instructions should begin 'Find someone who ... yesterday'.

5.3 Airport lounge

LEVEL

Elementary and above

TIME

5 minutes

MATERIALS

Small job cards for each student (see over)

PREPARATION

Prepare sets of job cards for your students. Examples are given below, but you will have to adapt these according to the number and level of students you have in the class and the number you want in each group.

PROCEDURE

1 Give out the cards at random to the students and tell them that they are in an airport lounge and have to find the other people they will be travelling with. They do not know what they look like, but they know what they do.

2 When they have found all the other members of their group, they should sit down with them.

REMARKS

This is a useful game for getting the students into groups in preparation for another activity.

SAMPLE JOB CARDS

> You are a TV cameraman travelling to Borneo to make a wildlife film. You are meeting the other members of the TV team in the departure lounge. Find the other members of the TV team.

> You are a TV producer travelling to Borneo to make a film about wildlife. You are meeting the other members of the TV team in the departure lounge. Find the other members of your crew.

> You are a wildlife expert travelling to Borneo to make a TV film. You are meeting the other members of the TV team in the departure lounge. Find the people who will be travelling with you.

> You are a TV technician who is travelling to Borneo to make a film about wildlife. You are meeting the other members of the TV team in the departure lounge. Find the other members of the TV team.

Similar cards can be easily made for a tour group, a volleyball team, a chess team, the plane crew, a circus, etc.

5.4 Stations

LEVEL   Elementary

TIME   5 minutes

MATERIALS   Role card for each student

PREPARATION   Make paired role cards for the students as in the following example:

> **Stuart from New Zealand**
>
> You are supposed to be meeting someone at the station, but you don't know what he looks like. You do know that his name is Mike and he comes from Australia.

> **Mike from Australia**
>
> Someone is supposed to be meeting you at the station but you don't know what he looks like. You do know his name is Stuart and he comes from New Zealand.

PROCEDURE

1 Divide the class into two halves.

2 Give one half the 'meeting' cards and tell them they are on a station platform waiting for a train to come in. Give the other half the 'being met' cards and tell them that they are on a train. Someone is going to meet them at the station.

3 Create the station and the train.

4 Elicit such questions as: 'Excuse me, but is your name...?' 'Do you come from...?' 'Ah, pleased to meet you. I'm...' from the class.

5 Students should find their 'other half', using these questions, and go and sit down with them.

5.5 Picture sections

LEVEL

Elementary and above (depending on the complexity of the pictures)

TIME

5–10 minutes

MATERIALS

Magazine pictures

PREPARATION

Collect some magazine pictures and cut them into four quarters. You will need as many quarter-pictures as there are students in the class.

PROCEDURE

1 Give out the picture sections at random.

2 Ask the students to find the three people with the other parts of their picture. To do this, they must describe their pictures to each other without showing them to anyone.

3 When they have found each other, they should sit down in a group together.

Acknowledgement
I first learned this activity on a drama workshop run by Alan Maley.

5.6 Invitations

LEVEL   **Elementary**

TIME   **5 minutes**

MATERIALS   **Role cards for each student**

PREPARATION   Make paired role cards, for example:

> You are going to a party tonight. Find someone to go with you.

> You have nothing to do tonight. You'd love to go to a party, but you don't really want to go to a film or a concert.

> You are going to a rock concert tonight and have a spare ticket. Find someone to go with you.

> You have nothing to do tonight. You don't want to go to a party or a film. You'd like to go to a rock concert.

> You are going to a film tonight...

PROCEDURE   1 Give out the role cards at random.

2 Ask students to find someone to spend the evening with them.

3 When they have found someone, they should sit down together.

REMARKS   This game obviously practises 'I'm going to/Would you like to/I'd love to' as well as dividing students into pairs. The game is easily adaptable to dividing students into threes and fours instead of pairs. To do this, just write in three or four people who favour each social event.

6 Getting to know each other: humanistic exercises and personalized grammar

A group is more likely to be cohesive and work productively if its members know something about each other, and are willing to disclose information about themselves. Many materials are now available which invite students to draw on their own personal experience, talk about themselves, and share feelings. The 'humanistic' approach in particular takes, in the words of Moskowitz (1978), a 'concern for personal development, self-acceptance, and acceptance by others' as its central focus, and materials in the humanistic tradition, or those influenced by it, can promote friendship, good feeling, and co-operation, while providing good language practice.

There seem to be two ways to use humanistic activities: either in their pure form, as an end in themselves, to develop a positive attitude to self and others, in which case they are often used as warm-up activities or ice-breakers; or in a derived form, as a means to an end, where they are used either to provide general speaking practice, or to practise some specific language point.

Teachers constrained by a crowded syllabus or standard textbook may feel they have little time to incorporate humanistic or group dynamics exercises into their teaching for their own sake, but may nevertheless wish to use activities with a more personal and motivating focus, particularly if their textbook is rather dry, or concerned with the exploits of a fictional character who is not particularly interesting or relevant to the students. One good way of getting the best of both worlds, humanistic and linguistic, is to use 'personalized' grammar practice exercises, which often provide very concentrated practice of a grammatical point, but which have a personal focus.

It is impossible to give a large range of such exercises here, but I have included exercises on major tenses, and there are suggestions in the bibliography for further sources of similar activities. The exercises make use of traditional forms of grammar practice: drills, substitution tables, and completion exercises, as well as newer activities such as pair practice and games, but all have in common the use of a grammatical form to communicate personal information.

6.1 What are they up to now?

LEVEL	**Elementary**
TIME	**10 minutes**
LANGUAGE	**Present continuous**
PROCEDURE	**1** Ask the class to close their eyes and think about the members of their family. What are they all doing now? Ask them questions: 'What is your mother doing? Your father? Your sisters? Your brothers? Your aunt? and so on. They should not answer, but keep their eyes closed and try to picture what they are doing.
	2 Ask them to open their eyes and tell their partner what the different members of their family are probably doing at that moment.

6.2 How often?

LEVEL	**Elementary**
TIME	**10 minutes**
LANGUAGE	**Simple present**
MATERIALS	**Copies of chart below for each student** (or put it on the board for students to copy down)
PREPARATION	Make copies of the chart if necessary.
PROCEDURE	**1** Give out copies of the chart or get students to copy it down from the board.
	2 Ask them to ask each other the questions and fill in the chart for their partner.
	3 When they have finished, ask them to write five sentences about their partner.
	4 Collect these in and use the information to make a wall-poster, for example:

Did you know...
- Ana never forgets things! (Do you believe her?)
- Danny never cries! (Do you believe him?)
- Felix quarrels with his sister almost every day.

CHART

How often do you:	very often	often	sometimes	rarely	never
cry	_____	_____	_____	_____	_____
laugh	_____	_____	_____	_____	_____
quarrel with your sister/brother	_____	_____	_____	_____	_____
feel happy for no reason	_____	_____	_____	_____	_____
feel sad for no reason	_____	_____	_____	_____	_____
daydream	_____	_____	_____	_____	_____
forget things	_____	_____	_____	_____	_____
wish you were someone else	_____	_____	_____	_____	_____
get angry	_____	_____	_____	_____	_____
do silly things	_____	_____	_____	_____	_____
make mistakes	_____	_____	_____	_____	_____
really enjoy yourself	_____	_____	_____	_____	_____
change your mind	_____	_____	_____	_____	_____

6.3 Past confessions

LEVEL Elementary

TIME 10 minutes

LANGUAGE Simple past

MATERIALS Copy of the substitution table for each student
(see below; or put it on the board or OHP)

PREPARATION Make copies of the table as necessary.

PROCEDURE 1 Give out the copies of the table or put it on the board.

2 Ask a few questions from the table to individual students, then get students to work in pairs asking and answering the questions.

3 When they have finished, ask a few students to tell the class some interesting facts about their partner.

4 Then get each student to write five sentences about their partner.

Photocopiable © Oxford University Press

5 Collect them in and use the information to write a wall-poster (see example below).

SUBSTITUTION TABLE

Question: When did you	first last	smoke a cigarette? ride a bicycle? fall in love? drink coffee? go to the dentist? go abroad?	
Answer: I first . . . I last . . .	X	months weeks days years hours minutes	ago.

SAMPLE WALL-POSTER

SECRET CONFESSIONS OF CLASS 1

ANDREAS FIRST FELL IN LOVE WHEN HE WAS SIX!

JULIETTE LAST WENT TO THE DENTIST FIVE YEARS AGO!

ANTONIO FIRST SMOKED A CIGARETTE IN THE SCHOOL PLAYGROUND WHEN HE WAS TEN!

6.4 Class records

LEVEL Intermediate

TIME 20 minutes

LANGUAGE Present perfect

MATERIALS **Copy of the question sheet** (see below), **poster size piece of paper**

PREPARATION Copy the question sheet, adding or deleting questions as necessary, and cut it up so there is one question for each student. Prepare the poster.

PROCEDURE 1 Give each student one question.

2 Ask them to go around the class and find out how many times everyone in the class had done these things. They should keep a running total.

3 When they have all finished, collate the information and fill it in on the poster. Pin the poster up on the wall.

QUESTION SHEET

Find how how many times people in the group have flown in a plane.	Find out how many times people in the group have broken their legs.
Find out how many times people in the group have drunk champagne.	Find how how many times people in the group have been to a pop concert.
Find out how many times people in the group have been in hospital.	Find out how many countries people in the group have visited.
Find out how many times people in the group have travelled on board a ship.	Find out how many times people in the group have won something in a competition.
Find out how many times people in the group have passed an exam.	Find out how many pets people in the group have owned. What kind of pets?
Find out how many times people in the group have fallen in love.	Find out how many times people in the group have changed jobs.

SAMPLE POSTER

AS A GROUP WE HAVE:
FLOWN IN A PLANE 25 TIMES
BROKEN OUR LEGS 3 TIMES
DRUNK 18 GLASSES OF CHAMPAGNE
BEEN TO 32 POP CONCERTS
BEEN IN HOSPITAL 10 TIMES
VISITED 27 COUNTRIES
TRAVELLED BY SEA 21 TIMES
WON A COMPETITION 7 TIMES
PASSED 49 EXAMS
OWNED 16 CATS 8 DOGS 2 HAMSTERS 9 GOLDFISH
FALLEN IN LOVE 21 TIMES
AND CHANGED JOBS 11 TIMES

6.5 Magic moments

LEVEL	Intermediate
TIME	15 minutes
LANGUAGE	Past continuous
MATERIALS	Copy of the questionnaire for each student (or put it on the OHP or board)
PREPARATION	Make copies of the questionnaire as necessary.

PROCEDURE

1 Begin by asking the class if they have younger brothers or sisters. Ask those who have if they can remember where they were and what they were doing when someone told them they had a new little baby brother or sister.

2 Then give out the questionnaire or write it up on the board or OHP for students to copy. See if students can think of more questions.

3 Ask them to ask each other the questions in pairs.

4 When students have finished, ask them each to tell the class one interesting fact about their partner.

SAMPLE QUESTIONNAIRE

MAGIC MOMENTS

Can you remember what you were doing when:

- your first tooth fell out?
- you first realized you could read?
- your parents told you you had a baby brother or sister?
- someone invited you out on your first date?
- you were offered your first job?
- you first understood what people were saying in English?

6.6 Group predictions

LEVEL

Intermediate

TIME

20 minutes

LANGUAGE

Will, future continuous, future perfect

PROCEDURE

1 Ask everyone in the class to imagine what the other people in the class will all be doing in ten years' time.

2 Ask them to write a prediction for everyone else in the group, plus one for themselves.

3 When they have finished, you can either ask them to read out their predictions, or pin them on the wall and let everyone go round and read them.

7 I did it your way: empathy activities

Members of a group are more likely to have a sympathetic and harmonious relationship if they make an attempt to understand each others' feelings and points of view. Many EFL activities now invite students to tell each other about their personal tastes, opinions, lifestyle, and background, and this usually has a very positive effect both on individual motivation and on group dynamics, as well as providing excellent language practice. But these activities largely focus on the simple transfer of information, rather than on the use of this information to increase understanding of others. Students will probably be more interested in talking about themselves than in hearing about their partner, partly for the natural human reason that one's own preoccupations are always more interesting than other people's, and partly because students tend to regard such activities primarily as a chance to practise their own speaking skills; they rarely seem to regard listening to another foreign student as very good language practice. The activities in this section go a little further than the normal personal information transfer activities in inviting the students to complete questionnaires, or write autobiographies not from their own point of view, but as if they were someone else. They are asked to empathize with another student, that is, to step into their shoes and see things through their eyes for a while. The act of putting yourself in another's place and looking at things from their point of view leads to a more direct and immediate understanding than the act of listening to and interpreting their words from your own viewpoint. It also provides a novel variation for students who have got used to filling in questionnaires and asking each other questions, though like any new activity it will rapidly become stale if it is used too often. 'Not another boring old dictation!' can just as easily become 'You're not asking us to empathize *again* are you!' These activities may be useful to try with a group whose problem is that they know each other too well and feel they have no information gaps left to fill. They are a challenge to see how well the students really know each other!

7.1 I am you

LEVEL Lower-intermediate and above

TIME 20–30 minutes

MATERIALS **One completion sheet for each student** (see below)

PROCEDURE 1 Divide the students into pairs.

2 Give each a copy of the completion sheet. Ask them to fill it in, not for themselves, but for their partner. However, they may not communicate with their partner while completing the sentences, but must do it by empathizing with their partner and imagining what he or she would reply.

3 When they have finished, students should compare their answers, commenting on their accuracy.

COMPLETION SHEET

I AM YOU

Imagine you are your partner and complete the sentences.

I like the colour _____ because _____ .

My favourite time of day is _____ .

When I was at school I used to _____ _____ .

I enjoy _____ .

I particularly dislike _____ .

The kind of music I like best is _____ .

I sometimes worry about _____ .

My biggest fear is _____ .

My ambition is to _____ .

I like people who _____ .

People like me because _____ .

REMARKS This activity obviously produces more accurate answers if students know each other fairly well, but it can also be used as an introductory activity with students who have only just met, when it becomes more of a guessing game.

7.2 If I were you

LEVEL	**Intermediate and above**
TIME	**15–20 minutes**
MATERIALS	**Questionnaire for each student**
PROCEDURE	**1** Seat students in pairs, preferably back to back so that they cannot see what their partner is writing.

2 Give one copy of the questionnaire to each student and ask them to fill it in as if they were their partner. However, they may not consult or confer with their partner during the exercise, but should complete the questionnaire with what they feel would be their partner's most probable responses.

3 When they have finished, ask them to turn to face each other and to compare their answers, commenting on their accuracy.

QUESTIONNAIRE

IF I WERE YOU

Complete the sentences as if you were your partner.

If I found some money in the street I would _____ .

If I saw a rat in the bedroom, I would _____ .

If I could travel anywhere in the world, I would _____
_____ .

My idea of a good evening out would be to _____ .

If I won a lot of money I would _____ .

A perfect day for me would be one where _____ .

If a hot air balloon landed in my garden, and the balloonist said 'Come for a ride!', I would _____ .

If someone invited me to join the crew in a Round-the-World yacht race I would _____
_____ .

If someone offered me the chance to work abroad for a year I would _____
_____ .

If I had the choice between an interesting but badly-paid job and a more boring but well-paid job I would _____ .

7.3 Ghostwriters

LEVEL　　　　　Lower-intermediate and above

TIME　　　　　One lesson

MATERIALS　　　Paper and pen for each student

PROCEDURE　　　1 Seat the students in pairs, or ask them to stand in a circle facing each other in pairs.

2 Tell them that they have five minutes to find out as much as possible about each other. They can do this in whatever way they like: either by having two and a half minutes of questions each, or by asking alternate questions. They can ask about anything at all to do with the other person's family, age, lifestyle, habits, job, likes and dislikes, or hobbies.

3 When the time is up, ask them to return to their places and to write their partner's autobiography: that is, they should write *as if they were the person they have just interviewed writing about him/herself*. They may, of course, put in all the facts their partner has just told them, but they may also put in other things which their partner may not have told them, but which they have observed, for example: 'I am quite a shy person, but I have a lovely sense of humour and when I get to know people I can be very witty'. They may also put in things which they do not know to be true, but which they imagine would be true, for example: 'I am a good husband and always do the washing-up'. All insertions of this kind should, of course, be positive—negative additions are to be discouraged.

4 When everyone has finished, pin the 'autobiographies' up round the wall and ask students to walk around and see if they can identify themselves!

7.4 How did it feel?

LEVEL　　　　　Intermediate and above

TIME　　　　　One lesson

MATERIALS　　　Paper and pen for each student

PREPARATION　　Find a suitable anecdote (see below).

PROCEDURE　　　1 Tell the class an anecdote about an incident in your life which caused you a variety of emotions, for example, fear, anger, embarrassment, or shame. An example is given below. While you tell the anecdote do not mention at any point how you felt, but just give the bare bones of the story.

2 Then tell the story again. This time ask the students to close their eyes and imagine themselves in your place. Stop at strategic points and ask them how they feel.

3 Then ask the students individually to think of an incident in their life that caused them some strong emotions. Give them a little time to think of one and to make notes if they wish.

4 Ask them to tell their story to a partner, as you did, without mentioning how they felt about the incident, merely stating what happened. The partner should listen, with eyes closed, imagining the events are happening to him/her.

5 Finally, ask each student to write their partner's story in the first person as if it happened to them, putting in the feelings. Pin the stories up around the wall for everyone to read.

REMARKS

Some students, for instance refugees learning ESL, may have had truly traumatic experiences, so you should know something of your class's background before selecting this activity.

SAMPLE STORY

I was living in France with my husband. Two friends came to stay with us * and we all went skiing for the weekend in a small village called Artouste. It had been snowing and the road above Artouste was closed. * The next day, the road was clear and we decided to go up the mountain in a cable car. * At the top, there was a small train that went round the mountain to a café. There was fog that day and we could not ski, * so we bought tickets for the train. As the train came out of a little tunnel, there was an avalanche * and the train came off the track. * The driver told us to carry our skis to the café. * We all followed the railway track, which had high walls of ice on each side. My husband and I walked behind our friends, and stopped to tie our skis onto our backs. Our friends disappeared in the fog in front of us. * As we came close to the cafe, we heard a terrible noise. * In the fog, we saw something coming towards us. * It was a huge snow plough with four long blades turning round on the front. * We were trapped on the railway track between the walls of ice. Where could we go? * I tried shouting but the snow plough was too noisy. * In the end, we stood against the wall and made ourselves as flat as possible. Would there be enough room for the snow plough to pass us? * It was coming nearer and nearer. * Suddenly, the driver saw us and stopped the engine. * We were very pleased to find our friends in the cafe, * and we all ordered brandies although it was only 9 o'clock in the morning. *

*=suitable place to stop and ask for feelings.

7.5 A day in your life

LEVEL

Lower-intermediate and above

TIME

One lesson

MATERIALS

Paper and pen for each student

PROCEDURE

1 Seat students in pairs or ask them to stand in a circle facing each other in pairs.

2 Tell them that they may ask five and only five questions about their partner's daily life: their age, job, journey to work or school, routine, and evening pastimes, for example.

3 When they have asked and answered their questions, ask them to sit down again or to move to a different place if they are seated in pairs. They should then write 'A Day in the Life' of their partner in the first person, as if they were their partner. They should use the information they got from their partner as a springboard, but can use their imagination and powers of empathy to fill in details they do not know. They should try to imagine what life is actually like for their partner and how he/she feels about it.

4 When they have finished, pin the decriptions round the room and invite students to walk around and see if they can identify themselves.

8 A sense of belonging: whole group identity activities

For a group to be harmonious and cohesive, it must have a definite sense of itself as a group, and the individuals who comprise it must have a sense of belonging to the group as well as a sense of their place within it. Very successful groups seem to build up a kind of group mythology, sometimes giving themselves names and inventing characteristics for themselves. In the 'real world' this can have negative effects (Hell's Angels or Skinheads, for example) or positive effects (for example, Greenpeace, Monty Python, Robin Hood and his Merry Men). In the classroom things rarely go so far (though I remember one class who christened themselves Snow-White and the Seven Dwarfs—and behaved accordingly), but all successful classes have one thing in common: the individuals in the class have a positive self-image and a strong sense of identity, maybe even a slight tendency to mythologize themselves, not as individuals so much as as a group. This warm, positive group feeling creates a supportive and enthusiastic atmosphere which is conducive to learning, so it is worth fostering. Obviously, there are limits to what the teacher can do, as the creation of a successful 'group legend' depends ultimately on the individuals in the group and the chemistry between them. But if we examine different types of classroom activity in terms of their effects on group dynamics rather than their teaching content, we see that some exercises, such as opinion gap activities, are designed to highlight individual differences, whereas others may be instrumental in bringing people together and creating a group atmosphere.

The activities in this section are designed to give the group this kind of positive self-image and sense of identity, as well as to give the individual student a sense of belonging to the group. They may be used throughout the course, though the first three are better used in the first couple of weeks, when students are still unacquainted with each other and it is important to establish the beginnings of a group identity. The last two are better used a little way into the course, when students know each other rather better.

8.1 Group history

LEVEL

Lower-intermediate and above

TIME

One lesson

MATERIALS

A very large sheet of paper for a wall chart, a small piece of paper for each student

PREPARATION

Find out how old the oldest student in the class is. Divide the number of years since they were born by the number of students in the class to give you a time period for each student. For example, if your oldest student is 30 and you have 15 students in the class, you will have 15 time periods of 2 years. Assign a time period to each student by writing dates on the top of each small piece of paper, for example, 1959–1960, 1961–1962. Then make a time chart on the large piece of paper, by writing the years in order down one side.

PROCEDURE

1 Give out the small pieces of paper, one to each student.

2 Tell them that they are all researchers working on a history of the life of the group, and that they are personally responsible for finding out what happened in the group life in the years assigned to them. To do this they should get up and move around the room, asking everyone else in the class what was the most memorable thing that happened to them in each of the years they are responsible for. They should write the answers down on the paper. Demonstrate how to do this first by asking a couple of students yourself 'What was the most important thing that happened to you in 1971, Carlos? Can you remember?' 'Yes, I got a bicycle for my birthday.' 'What about you, Anna? What happened to you in 1972?' 'I was born!' (If they can't remember anything, it doesn't matter.)

3 When everyone has collected their information, ask them to sit down again. Then compile the group history by asking them to report back. Write down the information they have collected on the time chart.

SAMPLE TIME CHART

> 1959 Akiko was born
> 1960 Akiko's family moved to Tokyo. Tomas was born.
> ....
> 1970 Akiko's brother was born. She felt very jealous! Tomas fell in love with the girl next door, who had a blonde pony-tail. Carlos got a bicycle for his seventh birthday, Anne-Marie started school and didn't like it. Kurt's grandmother came to live with them. Sergio broke his leg and spent four weeks in hospital. Sonia was born. Alicia was conceived.

VARIATION

If you have a large class, and the process of writing everything down as students report their findings seems rather laborious, you can give each student a strip of paper and ask them to write their own findings on it. Then paste these up on the wall chart.

REMARKS

1 If your class is a manageable size, the first method is better from the point of view of group atmosphere, as everyone is involved in the enterprise together, and it gives them an opportunity for interaction and discussion. You can also ask for additional detail, for example, 'What happened in 1970, Peter?' 'Akiko's little brother was born.' 'How did you feel about that, Akiko?' 'Very jealous!'

2 The students who researched time periods early on in the group's history will have less to report. You can give them something to do by asking them to take over the job of writing in the data on the chart once you have filled in a couple of lines to show them what to do.

3 With a large class of young learners, it will be impractical to divide the oldest pupil's age by the number of pupils, so divide the class into groups and give each group a time period to research.

8.2 Group profile

LEVEL

Lower-intermediate and above

TIME

One lesson

MATERIALS

A small piece of paper and a large sheet of paper for everyone in the group

PREPARATION

Think of one topic, such as 'likes', 'pet hates', 'hobbies', or 'fears', for everyone in the group, and write one title on each small sheet of paper. More suggestions for topics are given below.

PROCEDURE

1 Give one topic paper to every student in the group.

2 Tell them that they are going to conduct a survey about various aspects of the group's behaviour. Ask them to think of five questions on their topic to ask the others in the group. (If you have a very small class, you may like to increase the number of questions; if you have a large class, you may like to decrease the number.)

3 Then ask them to prepare a chart with names of students vertically down one side and the questions across the top. Give them an example, such as:

FEARS					
	Flying	Spiders	Old age	Snakes	Dentists
Alicia					
Johann					
Kurt					
Danny					

4 Then ask them all to get up and move around the class, putting their questions to everyone in the class.

5 When they have finished, ask them to sit down, and give everyone a large sheet of paper and some coloured pens or crayons.

6 They should now make a poster to portray their findings in whatever form they choose. If they are scientifically minded, this could take the form of a bar graph or pie chart. If they are artistically minded, they may like to draw pictures or cartoons. They may choose to write their findings in a list, or they could write a newspaper article. Alternatively, they may just select the single most startling fact and write it in capitals across the page.

7 When they have finished, ask them to pin up their posters around the room, and allow time for everyone to go round reading them.

8 Ask for reactions. Students may comment, for example: 'I never thought so many other people would be afraid of flying', or 'We're a very sporty group'.

Suggestions for topics: sports, travel, getting up, food, families, bad habits, colours, things that make you happy, things that worry you, entertainment, schooldays, childhood, the future, hopes and ambitions, values, money, love.

8.3 Rainy Sunday Shock Horror: a group newspaper

LEVEL

Intermediate and above

TIME

One lesson

MATERIALS

A very large sheet of paper for a wall newspaper, coloured pens, a small sheet of paper and a long strip of paper for each student (newspaper column size), scissors, paste

PREPARATION

Write an 'interview' task for each student at the top of each small sheet of paper. Suggestions for tasks are given below.

PROCEDURE

1 Give out the interview tasks.

2 Tell the class they are newspaper reporters and their job is to find out what people in the class did at the weekend. They should go around the class and 'interview' people according to the task on their sheets, making a note of the answers.

3 When they have finished, give out the strips of paper and coloured pens and ask them to write a report on their findings in the most sensational way possible, no matter how mundane their findings. They should write across the strips of paper, as in a newspaper column. They should give their report an eye-catching headline, for example *Rainy Sunday Shock Horror: Whole Class Stays Home/Johann Seen At Disco With Blonde Lovely/Roberto Goes Bowling, Comes Home Drunk*.

4 When they have finished, get them to arrange their columns on the wall newspaper, and to paste them in place. Decide together on a title for the newspaper and pin it up on the wall for everyone to read.

Ideas for interview tasks:

Find out what time everyone in the class went to bed on Saturday night. Who went to bed latest?

Find out how many people did their homework this weekend.

Find out what time everyone got up on Sunday morning. Who got up latest?

Did anyone see anyone else from the class doing anything this weekend?

How many people watched TV on Friday night?

Who went to the disco this weekend?

What did most people eat for breakfast on Sunday morning?

What did everyone do on Sunday afternoon?

What was the most popular activity on Friday night?

How many people went shopping? Who spent the most money?

You can also give tasks to find out information about specific students, for example: 'What did Almudena do on Saturday?' but in this case, make sure you cover everyone in the class.

REMARKS   This is obviously an activity for the first lesson on Monday morning. The Monday after the first weekend of term is a good time to use it, when some of the ice broken in the first week may have begun to form again after the group have spent a weekend apart.

8.4 Group portrait with melon

LEVEL   Elementary and above

TIME   One lesson (or parts of lessons on two separate days)

MATERIALS   Camera and film, preferably Polaroid (if available), dressing-up clothes (or selection of hats), an intriguing object such as a melon

PROCEDURE   1 Bring the clothes, object, and camera into the class. Ask each student to select an item or items of clothing to dress up in.

2 Ask them to imagine what kind of character they have become in their new clothes (for example, an old lady in a shawl, a businessman in a bowler hat).

3 Then ask them to come to the front of the class and assemble for a group portrait. They should strike poses according to the kind of character they imagine they are.

4 Give the object to the person in the middle of the front row to hold, and take a number of photos of the group: half as many as there are students in the class. If you have a Polaroid, you can proceed immediately with the next stage, but if you have an ordinary camera, you will have to do the next stage when the prints are ready.

5 Divide the students into pairs and give each pair a photo.

6 Ask them to imagine who all those people are, and invent the story behind why they were all there at that particular time with that strange object.

7 When the stories are ready, pin them up around the class, together with the photos.

REMARKS

1 Although this activity, unlike the others in this section, is based on fantasy not reality, the act of taking a photo of the whole group, together with the various inventive theories suggested for why they should all be together, is an activity that contributes greatly to the students' sense of themselves as a group.

2 If no camera is available, take an imaginary photo using elaborate procedures. The students stay in their photo groups for stage 6.

8.5 Group advert

LEVEL

Lower-intermediate and above

TIME

One lesson

MATERIALS

Selection of advertisements from magazines, a questionnaire for each student, a pile of small slips of paper for each pair of students, a large sheet of paper and coloured pens for each pair

PREPARATION

Cut out a number of advertisements from magazines and prepare a scanning questionnaire based on the qualities of the products advertised, for example: 'Which powder "washes whitest"?' 'What tastes delicious and is so easy to prepare?' 'What is so good about *Easicleen*?'

PROCEDURE

1 Pin the advertisements up around the classroom (before the students arrive if possible).

2 As they arrive, give each a questionnaire and ask them to find the answers and write them on the questionnaire as quickly as possible. They should sit down when they have finished.

3 When everyone is sitting down, go through the answers.

4 Then divide the students into pairs and give each pair a pile of small slips of paper.

5 Give them a time limit (2 or 3 minutes) and ask them to brainstorm, as quickly as possible, all the positive superlative adjectives that could describe the class. They should do this by writing each word on one of the slips of paper as it occurs to them. It is important to work as quickly as possible to keep up the flow of adjectives.

6 When the time limit is up, collect suggestions and write them on the board.

7 Then give out the large sheets of paper and coloured pens.

8 Tell them you are going to leave them, and they have to persuade another teacher to take over the class. The other teachers are all very busy, so they will have to entice them by telling them what a wonderful class they are and what a rewarding experience it will be to teach them. Ask them in their pairs to design an advert for the class.

9 When each pair has finished, pin their adverts up around the classroom and let everyone go around and read them.

8.6 One big family

LEVEL

Lower-intermediate and above

TIME

20 minutes

MATERIALS

None necessary, camera and film optional

PROCEDURE

1 If you have a fairly large classroom with movable furniture, clear a space in the centre. If this is impossible, use the board.

2 Draw a rough family tree either on the board or on the floor, with chalk. The tree should be a rough outline of the branches of a family, but without too much specific detail of how many people there are in each generation.

3 Ask the students to think of the class as a big family, and invite them to position themselves on the family tree according to how they perceive their role in the group, either by coming and standing in that position on the floor, or by writing in their name on the board. You can give an example and encourage them to begin, by placing yourself on the tree and saying, for example, 'I'm the grandfather: I sit around and tell everyone else to do all the work' or 'I'm the bossy old aunt. I'm always nagging you to get things done and telling you how you should behave'.

4 When everyone is in place, you can round off the activity by asking everyone to pose in their roles for a class (family) photo.

REMARKS

This is an activity for when the class are fairly familiar with each other and a group atmosphere has been established. It's probably best kept on a humorous level—set the tone by your characterization of yourself. It is fun if the activity is rounded off by a photo. If you prefer to take the activity to a deeper level, you can have some discussion on people's perception of their roles and how they feel about them, but you could get into deep water this way. If your class, despite all your efforts, have less-than-friendly feelings towards each other, don't even attempt the activity. Families can be cosy and supportive but they can equally well be seed-beds of tension and conflict!

9 Establishing trust: trust- and confidence- building activities

Feelings of insecurity play a large part in the build-up of a negative group atmosphere. The vicious circle goes like this: you aren't sure what other people think of you, so you won't give anything away for fear of criticism or a hostile reaction, or simply of looking silly in public; the less you give away about yourself, the more unsure you are about what other people may be thinking and feeling. If this process is going on simultaneously in the minds and hearts of ten or twenty people in your classroom, the result will be the kind of introverted, taciturn, ungenerous group that so many teachers complained of in their responses to our questionnaire. The members of such a group are not necessarily hostile or aggressive. They may just be insecure and lacking in confidence. Understanding this is important, because their reactions can easily be mistaken for hostility, and hostility tends to breed more hostility, so that a group that starts off merely lacking self-confidence can easily slide into negativity and antagonism.

To counteract this, it is important to establish a climate of trust among the members of the group, so that they can feel confident enough to say and do things in front of others without fear. This is particularly important in the foreign language classroom as it is very easy to feel stupid when struggling to speak a foreign language. Obviously, the attitude of the teacher is vital here. Particularly with beginners' groups, who are especially vulnerable to insecurity and nervousness, it is important for the teacher to have a reassuring, encouraging, and comforting manner. But it is perhaps even more important for the group members to feel support, encouragement, and acceptance from the group. You can be as supportive as you like, but if J knows (or feels—it doesn't have to be true!) that every time he opens his mouth he will be sneered at by the rest of the group, then he will not be inclined to open his mouth very much.

This section introduces some activities that may help to build up a classroom climate where learners accept and trust each other and have enough confidence in themselves and in each other to be able to express themselves without fear of making fools of themselves. Even better, they may feel able to go ahead and make fools of themselves and thoroughly enjoy it! The techniques are derived from drama activities where they are used to build confidence in the individual and a sense of solidarity in the group, and most are, at least in the initial stages, non-verbal. It is easier to establish a relationship of physical trust between people than to get them to trust each other with things they say. Out of this physical trust will come an emotional trust, which may finally be put into words.

9.1 Falling

LEVEL All

TIME 10–15 minutes

PROCEDURE

1 Clear a large space in the middle of the room.

2 Ask students to stand together in pairs, with one student's back towards the other's front.

3 Ask this student to fall backwards towards their partner, who should be ready to catch them.

4 Then they reverse roles.

5 Divide the class into groups of about ten to fifteen. Ask the groups to stand in tight circles, facing inwards.

6 Ask one student to stand in the centre and fall backwards so that he or she is caught and supported by the other students in the circle, who should push him or her gently forwards or sideways so that others in the circle can catch and push him or her on.

7 Repeat until everyone in the class has had a turn, though if anyone really does not want to do it, you should not force them.

See next activity for Remarks.

9.2 Blind trust

LEVEL All

TIME 5–10 minutes

PROCEDURE

1 Clear the furniture from the centre of the room, but leave a few chairs scattered around the cleared area: enough to act as obstacles, but not enough to impede progress seriously.

2 Ask the students to get into pairs.

3 One in each pair should close their eyes and the other should guide them round the room, taking care to negotiate the obstacles.

4 After a few minutes they reverse roles.

5 Then ask all the students except one to sit down around the edge of the room. The student in the centre should close his or her eyes and begin to walk, while the others call out directions and instructions to help him or her avoid bumping into the obstacles.

6 Repeat with everyone in the class.

REMARKS

Activities 9.1 and 9.2 are used as warm-up activities in drama to create trust and release inhibitions. By encouraging students to trust each other physically, that is, to let themselves go and put themselves in somebody else's power, a strong feeling of closeness and trust can be achieved.

VARIATION

Words are not really necessary here, but I sometimes round off these two activities by asking students to sit in a circle on the floor and talk about their reactions.

You can ask questions such as:
- How did you feel when you fell?
- How did you feel when 'blind'?
- How did you feel when you had to catch someone?
- How did you feel when you had to guide someone?
- How did you feel towards the person who caught or guided you?
- How did you feel towards the person you caught or guided?
- What analogies can you make between those two activities and your own lives—are you in the catcher/guider relationship with anyone? Are you in the falling/blind relationship with anyone?
- Can you make any analogy between the two exercises and language learning?

Students are usually anxious to share their reactions and answers can be very interesting. The extension to this exercise has the effect of turning the relationship of physical trust into a verbal one.

9.3 Look after it for me

LEVEL

All

TIME

5–10 minutes

PROCEDURE

1 Clear a space in the middle of the room and ask students to stand in two lines facing each other.

2 Ask them to close their eyes and think of something that is precious to them. This can be an object they cherish or something more abstract like freedom or family life or the view from a window. It may help to play some quiet music.

3 Then ask the students to imagine they have to leave this thing for a while, and they are giving it to someone they trust to look after it until they come back.

4 Ask the students in one line to step forward and mime handing over the object or concept (obviously if it is an object they are handing over, they can be literal about its weight and size; if it is a concept they will have to be more imaginative).

5 The student receiving the precious object should handle it very carefully and show their partner how they would keep it safe.

6 Then they reverse roles.

7 When they have finished, ask them to explain to each other what it was they were entrusting to the other person and why it is so precious.

8 Finally, you can sit them round in a circle and ask everyone to tell the others what they were entrusted with and to describe how they felt on receiving it. The owners can describe how it felt to give it up to their partner.

REMARKS

This can also be done with real objects with Elementary students.

VARIATION

1 Proceed as for stages 1–3, except this time ask students to imagine that they are entrusting their partner with a secret.

2 They should mime the secret as a small object that they are handing into their partner's care. Their partner should tuck it away somewhere safe, giving reassurance that it will be kept.

3 Then ask students to change partners.

4 Their new partner should try to persuade them to give up the 'secret'; they should refuse adamantly and on no account give in.

5 When this is over, you can ask the students to sit round in a circle and talk about their feelings:

- How did they feel when handing over the secret?
- How did they feel when their partner received it and put it away?
- How did they feel when their partner was being persuaded to give up a secret?
- How did they feel when he or she refused?
- How did they feel when receiving the secret?
- How did they feel when being persuaded to give it up?

9.4 Promises promises

LEVEL

Lower-intermediate and above

TIME

15 minutes

MATERIALS

Paper and pen for each student

PROCEDURE

1 Ask students individually to think of two things: one should be something the rest of the class can do to help them and give them confidence (this can be something the class are doing already, or something they would like them to do); the other should be something they can do to help the rest of the class and give them confidence. They should be prepared to promise to do one, in return for the other.

2 When they are ready, sit them in a circle and begin the exercise yourself by promising to do something and asking if they will do something for you. For example: 'I promise never to get impatient if you don't understand something but to try and explain things as clearly and as carefully as I can. Can you promise never to lose your lovely sense of humour?'

3 Go round the circle in this way. If students think a promise is unreasonable or they feel they can't guarantee to keep it, they should say so honestly, and negotiate for easier terms!

REMARKS

This can be a very revealing exercise: students very often do not realize what they can do, or are doing already, to help class confidence, and it helps them to see how interdependent they—and you—are.

9.5 Silly walks

LEVEL

Lower-intermediate and above

TIME

10 minutes

PROCEDURE

1 Clear a large space in the centre of the room.

2 Ask the students to begin walking round.

3 As they do so, ask them to walk in different ways: on a sandy beach, on a hot surface with bare feet, in ski boots, on ice, in deep snow, in high-heeled shoes, in shoes that hurt, in shoes that are too big, through a river, paddling in the sea, and finally in deep mud.

4 Ask them to imagine they have got stuck in the mud and can only pull one leg out with great difficulty. As soon as they put their leg down again, it gets stuck again.

5 Ask them to wave to a friend and ask for help. (Designate half as friends and half as stick-in-the-muds.) But as their friends come to help them, they get stuck too. Stickily, they try to help each other to get out of the mud to drier land.

REMARKS

This activity has a twofold purpose: it aims to develop trust by getting students to help each other out of a sticky predicament, and it aims to release inhibitions by putting everyone in the same silly situation. The activity can lead to a lot of laughter. I once had a whole class that decided almost simultaneously that they would all overbalance into the mud together. When you have had a whole class rolling on the floor in giggles, it is difficult for anyone in the group to feel inhibited about making a fool of themselves in public again!

Sources and acknowledgements
'Falling', 'Blind trust', and 'Silly walks' are familiar warm-up techniques used in drama workshops. I first learned them from drama classes at university, and learned of their EFL use from Alan Maley.

10 Staying positive: encouraging positive feelings

The alarming thing about negative feelings is that once they develop they are very tenacious. Negativity has a very powerful attraction. For some reason, criticism is easier to voice than praise, dissatisfaction than satisfaction. People often seem to find a certain solidarity in complaining and once negative feelings get a grip on people it is easy for the group to descend into a rapid downward spiral of negativity. It is especially easy for foreign students studying in Britain to develop these feelings: alone, away from home and everything they find familiar, they can feel alienated and vulnerable. If you find yourself suddenly in an environment where all the rules you are used to have changed, and everything you previously took for granted is no longer valid, then it is easy to feel threatened. You may tend to safeguard your own sense of reality and what you feel to be right by reacting negatively to everything in the alien culture and its language, including sometimes the teaching methods, if they are very different to the methods you are used to.

But there is another very powerful source of negative feelings in a group. Students may feel uncertain about themselves, their place in the group, and their learning abilities. This can result in timidity and a lack of self-confidence; it can also lead to a defensive reaction towards others in the group.

A positive attitude towards oneself as a learner, towards the learning process, and towards the language and culture being studied are obviously essential if any progress is to be made. If you have little faith in your own ability to learn, little enjoyment of or feeling for the language, and feel alienated by and resentful of the culture, you will not be highly motivated to learn. Once a group begins to spiral into negativity, it is hard to stop it. Personally, I have had very little success with trying to sort out students' negative feelings and the reasons behind them by patient, rational discussion. This may be partly because analytic discussion of this kind tends to focus on the problem rather than on possible solutions, and thus ends up exacerbating what it set out to cure; and partly because such discussions tend to assume that these feelings are rational and can therefore be rationalized away, whereas attitudes to oneself and one's abilities, and to a foreign language and culture, are an emotional affair. Even if the student *knows* that a more positive attitude would be more beneficial, knowledge is not *feeling*.

The activities suggested in this section are therefore all affective in nature, and aim at building up and reinforcing positive feelings about one's self and one's abilities, about the language and culture, and about other people in the group. They are probably best used sprinkled throughout the course, rather than in a concentrated burst in a desperate attempt to stave off negativity, but may be particularly useful towards the middle of a term, when many otherwise happy and outgoing students experience a mid-term slump.

10.1 I like it when...

LEVEL

Elementary and above

TIME

15 minutes

MATERIALS

Paper and pen for each student, large sheet of paper for a wall-poster, coloured pens

PREPARATION

Write a large heading on the poster: 'I like it when...'

PROCEDURE

1 Ask students to close their eyes and think of things they have enjoyed or found interesting about being in an English-speaking country, or learning the language. These could be things that have happened to them or things they have noticed about the way people behave, or things they like about the language itself.

2 Give them a little time to think in peace, then ask them to join up with a partner and write as many endings to the sentence 'I like it when...' as they can, for example:

I like it when:
– people's voices go up when they ask a question
– shop assistants call me 'Duck'
– motorists stop for me at zebra crossings!

3 When people seem to be running out of ideas, collect the endings. You can do this either by asking them to call out what they have written and writing it up on the poster (my preference, for the sense of group involvement and shared experiences it gives) or by asking pairs to write their sentence endings on strips of paper and glue them to the poster. In either case, pin the poster up on the wall and leave it there. Students can then add to it as the term goes on.

Acknowledgement
I got this idea from an American co-teacher, Deborah Deborde Schulze, who had an exercise called 'Don't you hate it when...' which she used with high school students. I thought that as a group dynamics exercise it would be better to turn it on its head and give it a positive slant!

10.2 My English self

LEVEL

Intermediate and above

TIME

15–20 minutes

MATERIALS

A large sheet of paper for a poster

PREPARATION

Write a heading on the poster: 'My English self', and underneath that: 'In English I can...'

PROCEDURE

When you speak a foreign language you have in a sense to create a new personality for yourself. The 'I' you know in French or German will not be the same as your English 'I'. This can be an exciting and liberating prospect, but it can also be an intimidating one. This exercise aims to get students to recognize and enjoy their English self.

1 Ask students individually to write down five qualities they think they have, five qualities they definitely do not have, and five qualities they would like more of.

2 Then introduce the idea of the English self. Ask them to review the list, considering whether there are any differences when they are speaking English. Do they have more or less of any qualities? And, most important, given the freedom a new language brings to recreate themselves, what *could* they perhaps be in English?

3 Ask them to discuss these ideas in pairs.

4 Then ask for ideas from the group to complete the sentence you have written on the poster. Write their ideas up as they call them out.

5 Pin the poster on the wall so that students can add to it.

REMARKS

Some students may produce negative ideas at first, such as: 'In English I am shyer/less articulate.' Let them work through these in the pairwork phase, and come on to the idea of their potential English self and the liberation a new language offers: ideas students produce here are usually far more positive, for example: 'In English I can be funny/be creative/play a lot/swear more(!)' and so on.

10.3 Wanted: the perfect student

LEVEL	**Lower-intermediate and above**
TIME	**One lesson**
MATERIALS	**Two large poster-size pieces of paper**
PREPARATION	Copy the advertisement (see below) onto one poster, changing it to suit yourself and your class.
PROCEDURE	1 Pin the advertisement up on the board without commenting and let the students read it.

2 Ask them to write a letter of application for the job, extolling their own virtues. They can boast as much as they like!

3 When they have finished, they must find a referee. They should give the letter to their referee who should read it and write them a reference on the back, then hand it in. As in normal life, the applicant is not allowed to see the reference!

4 As you receive the letters, glue them to the second poster. Do this by folding over one corner, gluing the back, and attaching the paper by that corner. The letter of application should be on the front, so that readers will have to turn the letter over to see the reference.

SAMPLE ADVERT

Wanted!!!

The Perfect Student

Busy but affectionate teacher seeks ideal student to join hardworking group. The job is challenging, rewarding, and enjoyable. The successful applicant will be adventurous, sensitive, generous, talkative, uninhibited, punctual, tolerant, warm-hearted, witty, extremely hard-working, amusing, friendly, and willing to buy the drinks at Friday lunchtimes.

Hours of work: 9am–1am, Mondays to Sundays

Pay: None

REMARKS

I would not attempt this activity with a group who do not get on with each other, because in these circumstances it could be seen as rather aggressive or antagonistic. I would use it either (obviously) with a group who liked each other and had a good sense of humour, or to cheer up a group who basically work well together, but who may be feeling a bit low. Because the whole exercise is tongue-in-cheek, people feel able to list their good qualities, a task most people usually find rather hard or embarrassing. Provided the group is basically amicable, students will be pleasantly surprised at the nice things people write on their references. There may be some affectionate teasing, but mostly students write lovely things about each other. Again, the 'spoof' context makes them feel free to express praise and liking. The fact that the writers of references themselves have to have a reference written may also have something to do with it, but whatever the reasons, this exercise is a good morale-booster!

10.4 Medals

LEVEL

Elementary and above

TIME

15 minutes to one lesson (depending on the number in the class)

MATERIALS

'Medals' and pins, coloured felt-tip pens

PREPARATION

Make 'medals' out of coloured paper, following one of the outlines below. Prepare enough for every student in the class to have one to give each of the other students and one for themselves.

PROCEDURE

1 Make yourself a medal, saying 'Longsuffering Mother', 'Good Friend', or 'Patient Teacher', or some other quality you would like to congratulate yourself on. Wear it to class.

2 Explain to the students that you felt you weren't getting enough recognition, so you thought you'd award yourself a medal. Tell them you thought it was about time for a bit of general recognition all round, so you've decided on a merit awards ceremony.

3 Get students to sit in different corners of the room, so that they can work in secret, and give out the blank medals.

4 Ask them to make a medal for everyone in the class, honouring them for some quality they possess. When they've done one for everyone else, they can make one for themselves.

5 When everyone has finished, have a decoration ceremony with as much pomp and circumstance as possible, and solemn music if

practicable. Students should come forward one at a time to
receive all their decorations and when their chest is covered with
medals, they can pin their own on, explaining why they think
they deserve it.

MEDAL OUTLINES

REMARKS

The 'send-up' atmosphere makes it possible for people to
congratulate themselves and others and to express liking,
something we often feel too awkward and inhibited to do. This
activity creates a very pleasant—and frequently
hilarious—atmosphere.

Source
This idea came to me after a British Council teacher training
workshop in Calw, Germany, where the trainees made medals for
the tutors at the end of the course. Why not medals for
everyone?

10.5 Crazy compliments

LEVEL

Elementary and above

TIME

10 minutes

MATERIALS

Placard for each student (see below), pins

PROCEDURE

1 Give each student a placard and pin it to their backs. They
should not be allowed to see their own placard.
2 Ask them to mill around freely, obeying the instructions on
each other's backs.

**SAMPLE
PLACARDS**

10.6 Present-giving

LEVEL   All

TIME   10 minutes

PROCEDURE

1 Ask students to stand in two lines facing each other.

2 Ask them to imagine a present they would like to give to the person opposite them.

3 When they are ready, ask them to mime giving the present to the other person.

4 When they have given and received presents, ask them to tell their partners why they chose those particular gifts for them.

Source
This is a familiar drama workshop activity.

10.7 The negative feelings dustbin

LEVEL

Elementary and above

TIME

10 minutes

MATERIALS

Sheet of paper for each student, wastepaper basket

PROCEDURE

1 Give out the sheets of paper and tell the students this is an exercise to get rid of bad feelings (not to indulge them!).

2 Ask them to write down all the things they are feeling angry, depressed, or fed-up about in their present situation. These could be things to do with living away from home, or British people, the weather, themselves, or learning the language. Reassure them that no one will read what they have written, so they can feel free to write anything. They must begin writing when you say 'GO' and write without taking their pen from the paper for five minutes.

3 If they are still writing furiously after five minutes, give them a little longer to write themselves out.

4 Ask them to put their pens down and pass around the wastepaper basket. Students should crumple up their papers, enjoying the sensation, and fling them into the basket putting as much force and as much expression into the action as possible.

REMARKS

This is an exercise I have done with a basically fairly cheerful class who were undergoing the mid-term blues. I have also tried it myself when I was experiencing negative feelings towards the country I was living in. I am not sure it would work with a very negative group, as I think it gets rid of temporary grumpiness but not more deep-rooted feelings. It's nice to follow this exercise with one that creates warm emotions like 'Present-giving' (10.6).

11 Group achievements: product-orientated activities

Much work done in class is ephemeral: at the end of the lesson a lot of words have been spoken, and retained briefly, only to dissolve into the words of the next lesson and the one after that. This ephemerality is, of course, in the nature of language. Only at elementary level can language somehow be quantified in numbers of items learned, and each lesson seem a solid achievement, a definite step forward. At intermediate level and beyond, language is a very slippery thing to grasp. The frustration many learners feel at intermediate level stems from this feeling that language is eluding them; they want to grasp it, to hold it, and somehow to possess it. The emphasis on aural/oral skills in the classroom exacerbates this intangibility of language.

I have the feeling that a lot of tensions in groups, particularly at intermediate level where students are making the difficult transition from a situation where language can somehow be dealt out in chunks to a situation where language becomes altogether more insubstantial and progress cannot be measured so easily, may be due in part to this unsatisfied feeling, that is, the need to possess something that cannot be possessed. Group unity can dissolve as everyone makes their own individual bid for possession. This can be intensified by the fact that group- or pairwork can be inconclusive and open-ended if there is no satisfying goal or conclusion to a discussion or role play.

If there is a tangible product at the end of a lesson it tends to be a written one. But most written products are individual, and tend to be set for homework. Individual work is obviously a vital part of language learning, and I am not decrying it: quite apart from its obvious pedagogical necessity, it has the important psychological effect of giving students space, time to stand back from the group and the learning process, time for personal reflection, and time to process what they have learned in their own way. Giving the individual members of a group sufficient personal space is vital for group life since groups, like families, can be claustrophobic as well as supportive. However, if all language products are individually produced, this can have a negative effect on group life, by increasing fragmentation, particularly if homework is graded and the group members measure themselves against each other. If, in addition, most group- or pairwork done in class is inconclusive and open-ended, students may come to the conclusion that groupwork is insubstantial and unsatisfactory and that the real, concrete progress can only be achieved alone.

We can redress the balance somewhat by including in our teaching some activities which give the group a common task and lead to a group product. The activities suggested in this section are designed to give groups a common purpose that will lead to a recognizable, tangible achievement. The commonality of purpose demands support from group members for each other, and the fact that there is an end-product gives the group a feeling of satisfaction and a sense of pride in themselves as a group. Group products do not have to be written: they can be oral or visual, and they can range from lengthy and demanding projects taking a whole term, for example, the making of a video film, the performing of a drama show, or the production of a magazine, or even a short book, to shorter activities taking one lesson, or at most a whole morning. For reasons of space, only examples of short 'one-off' activities are included here; sources for lengthier projects are given in the bibliography.

11.1 'A partridge in a pear tree': a group song

LEVEL	**Intermediate and above**
TIME	**One lesson**
MATERIALS	**Copies of the words of the song, a recording of the song (or be prepared to sing it yourself with the students), copies of the first lines** (see below)
PREPARATION	Copy out and cut up the first lines so that there is one for each group of students; prepare copies of the words for each student, or write them on the board or OHP.
PROCEDURE	**1** Play or sing with the students the Christmas song 'A partridge in a pear tree' (words below).

2 Divide the students into groups of three or four and give them a first line, or let them choose one.

3 Ask them to continue the song. Help them to get the right rhythm by encouraging each group as they produce a line to hum or sing it to see if it fits. It is reasonably easy to get the rhythm if you stick to the pattern 'number–adjective–noun' for verses 2–5 and 'number–noun–verb (gerund)' for the last seven verses. However, don't discourage experiments!

4 When they have finished, you can all sing the songs!

The twelve days of Christmas

A partridge in a pear tree

On the first day of Christmas my true love gave to me
A partridge in a pear tree.

On the second day of Christmas my true love gave to me
Two turtle doves
And a partridge in a pear tree.

And so on until:
On the twelfth day of Christmas my true love gave to me
Twelve drummers drumming
Eleven pipers piping
Ten lords a-leaping
Nine ladies dancing
Eight maids a-milking
Seven swans a-swimming
Six geese a-laying
Five gold rings
Four calling birds
Three French hens
Two turtle doves
And a partridge in a pear tree.

Suggested first lines

In my first year of life, my parents gave to me...

In my first year at school, my teachers gave to me...

In the first week of term, my teacher gave to me...

On my first day at work, my bosses gave to me...

On the first day of April, the postman brought to me...

When I arrived in London, the customs took from me...
(change the towns in each verse, for example 'When I arrived in Rome...')

On the first day of my diet, I cooked myself for tea...

11.2 'Tonight at noon': a group poem

LEVEL	**Intermediate and above**
TIME	**One lesson**
MATERIALS	**Copy of the poem 'Tonight at noon' for each student** (or write it on the board or OHP for the class to copy)

Tonight at noon

Tonight at noon
Supermarkets will advertise 3d EXTRA on everything
Tonight at noon
Children from happy families will be sent to live in a home
Elephants will tell each other human jokes
America will declare peace on Russia
World War I generals will sell poppies in the streets on
    November 11th
The first daffodils of autumn will appear
When the leaves fall upwards to the trees

Tonight at noon
Pigeons will hunt cats through city backyards
Hitler will tell us to fight on the beaches and on the landing
    fields
A tunnel full of water will be built under Liverpool
Pigs will be sighted flying in formation over Woolton
and Nelson will not only get his eye back but his arm as well
White Americans will demonstrate for equal rights
in front of the Black House
and the Monster has just created Dr Frankenstein

Girls in bikinis are moonbathing
Folksongs are being sung by real folk
Artgalleries are closed to people over 21
Poets get their poems in the Top 20
Politicians are elected to insane asylums
There's jobs for everyone and nobody wants them
In back alleys everywhere teenage lovers are kissing
In broad daylight

In forgotten graveyards everywhere the dead will quietly
bury the living
and
You will tell me you love me
Tonight at noon

Adrian Henri

PROCEDURE

1 Ask the students to think of an unlikely prediction about themselves—something they would like to happen, but which probably won't: 'I will pass my exam', 'My boss will give me a pay rise', 'My boyfriend will ask me to marry him', and so on.

2 Ask the students to write their predictions on small pieces of paper, collect them up, and put them in a bag.

3 Now put up the following words on the board:

dead   madmen   Dr Frankenstein   daffodils
pigeons   war   noon   happy families   tunnel
sunbathing   unemployment

4 Ask the students to think of 'opposites' to these words. Some, like 'war' or 'dead', will be easy, others, like 'daffodils' or 'tunnel', will prove more difficult.

5 Then read the poem 'Tonight at noon' with the group. Ask them to find the 'opposites' in the poem.

6 When you have the list, ask them which words they associate with a positive meaning and which they find negative.

7 Then brainstorm a new list with the class, some students calling out words and some trying to find their opposites. (You can make this into a game with two teams if you like.)

8 Divide the words into positive and negative, according to the group consensus. Your list might end up something like this:

Negative	Positive
tunnel	light
snow	sand
valley	hill
torturer	saint
fish	bird
rain	sun
cloud	rainbow
work	play
sword	pen
gun	kiss
stone	flower
car horns	music

9 Now ask the students to choose a pair of words and write an unlikely prediction, linking them together, for example:

Fish will fly like birds.
All clouds will be rainbow-coloured.
Tunnels everywhere will be full of light.

10 Collect a few suggestions from the class and write them on the board.

11 Then put the students together in groups of three or four.

12 Pass round the bag containing the predictions they wrote earlier and ask each group to take one.

13 Tell them that this is the last line of their poem and put the first line on the board:

> Tomorrow morning at midnight . . .

The middle lines will be a collection of or selection from the lines they have just written, plus any more they can dream up.

14 The group task is to assemble all these raw materials into a poem.

A group poem can also be written using the poem 'A boy's head' printed at the front of this book.

1 Collect some magazine pictures of interesting faces and give one to each group.

2 Ask them to decide the person's age, job, personality, likes and dislikes, worries and fears.

3 Then read the poem with the students and ask each group to write a similar poem called, for example, 'A girl's head'/'An old man's head'/'A businessman's head'/'A baby's head', based on the character in their picture.

11.3 TV News

Lower-intermediate and above

One whole morning or afternoon

Video camera and console, copies of materials below, a selection of products for adverts, clothes and hats for dressing up. (If you have no video available, you can still do the programme 'live', with another class as a 'studio audience'.)

1 Tell the students they are a TV news team and they are at this minute in a studio putting together a half-hour local news programme which comes on the air at . . . (indicate time about 40 minutes before the end of the session).

The programme consists of:

– Local news (with interviews)
– Break for adverts
– Viewers' letters (with interviews)
– Weather forecast

2 Appoint a producer (choose a good organizer who is not too bossy), who will be in charge of co-ordinating the various parts of the programme and seeing that the programme goes out on time. If making a real video, appoint a camera operator to work with the producer (preferably someone who has some experience of using a video camera).

3 Ask the rest of the students to get into three groups: one to deal with news and weather, one to deal with viewers' letters, and one to deal with adverts. (If the groups are very uneven in size, you may have to do some redistributing.) Assign a 'newsdesk', a 'letterdesk', and an 'advertising executives' corner' in different parts of the room.

4 Explain what they have to do:

The newsdesk will receive news items, at about ten-minute intervals throughout the session. They should decide which items will feature in their programme (no need to use them all) and write a news bulletin for the newsreader to read out. The news items should be interspersed with interviews with people in the news. One member of the team should be the newsreader, and the rest can act as interviewers and interviewees for the main news stories. One member of the team is the weather presenter and should prepare a (funny) weather forecast for the end of the programme. He or she will need to draw a map with weather symbols on a part of the board.

The letterdesk will receive letters in two lots: first post and second post. They should select one or two to read out and do interviews with the letter-writers.

The ad team should choose four or five items (shampoo bottle, chocolate bar, window cleaner, toothpaste, etc.). They should design a series of adverts for the commercial break.

The producer and camera operator are responsible for general co-ordination. They will need to work out:
- the order of the items
- the timing of the items and the programme as a whole
- who is responsible for doing what and when
- where in the room the different parts of the programme will be filmed (it is a good idea to assign different areas to different sections: newsdesk, interviews, letters, ads, weather)
- design of the 'set' and backdrop (think what will be in the background when the newsreader, interviewers, etc. are being filmed)
- decide, with consultation, on a name for the programme
- title of the programme (design on piece of paper to be filmed close up, and/or on board behind newsreader) and signature tune.

5 When everyone is clear about their role, begin the simulation by giving the newsdesk the first two items, the letterdesk the first batch of letters (about two-thirds), and the advertising team their products.

6 Let them get on with it. Your role from now on is to:
- give out the news items at ten-minute intervals
- give the letterdesk the second post in about half an hour's time
- give support and advice to the producer and camera operator

— act as a language resource/walking dictionary/ideas consultant when needed
— make the clothes and dressing-up materials available when it looks as if people are beginning to practise their interviews.

7 When the teams are ready, begin filming. You will be able to allow a minute or so for rearrangement of furniture or people between each item, by pressing the pause button on the video camera, but lengthy delays should be avoided: there should be the sense of being 'on the air'.

Begin by filming the title on the paper or board, with the signature tune as background, then switch to the newsreader. As she or he is reading the first news items, the interviewer and interviewee for the first interview should be in place in the area of the room appointed by the producer for interviews, so that the camera operator can turn to them with a minimum of fuss. When they have done their interview and the camera swings back to the newsreader, the next pair should take their place for the second interview, and so on. Similarly, the letter reader should be in place to read the letters, ready for the camera. The adverts will probably be the most difficult, as there will be four or five short items in succession, and the camera operator will have to allow a pause between each item for rearrangement.

8 Arrange a time to 'broadcast' the news programme, and invite other classes in to watch. (Though your class may be impatient to watch the programme and insist on seeing it straight away!)

REMARKS

Don't worry too much if things are slow in starting—they will hot up later as the deadline approaches. I have never yet known a group who failed to deliver the goods, and on most occasions they surpassed their own expectations and surprised themselves with what they could do!

The materials given below are the ones we use in Devon. Obviously, it would be better to alter the names of the towns to ones in your own locality, and it will add zest if you personalize the materials further by writing in letters and news items of topical interest and include some 'in jokes'.

VARIATION

You could get the students to write letters and news items along these lines beforehand, for homework or as a separate task. Alternatively, this could be a follow-on activity.

MATERIALS _____ ### News items

POPSTAR ARRIVES

The famous popstar Gary Gleam is arriving in Torbay today. Crowds of fans are already waiting outside the Imperial Hotel where the star will be staying. He will be giving a concert at the Palace Theatre tonight. The concert is sold out and people have been paying up to £25 a ticket.

HOUSEWIFE WINS POOLS

A 67-year-old Exeter housewife, Mrs Betty Wallis, won £500,000 on the football pools today. Mrs Wallis lives on her own with her twenty-five cats.

UFO SIGHTED

Several people have reported seeing a mysterious silver object in the sky over Devon today. Some report a long, cigar-shaped object while others describe it as balloon-shaped. The object was sighted between 9 and 9:20 this morning and appeared to be travelling westwards very fast.

ACCIDENT

An accident occurred on the A380 today when a car collided with a lorry, causing a pile-up of 15 cars. Five people have been taken to Torbay Hospital, where their condition is said to be satisfactory.

LION ESCAPES

A lion escaped from Paignton Zoo this morning and raced along the beach causing panic to hundreds of holidaymakers. He was recaptured by zoo keepers in Thompson's the Butchers where he had just eaten forty steaks and three legs of lamb.

STRIKE

Workers at the Wonderland Toy Factory are on strike today in protest against a management decision to cut 300 jobs.

LIFESAVER

A language school student saved a girl from drowning today. *............ was taking a trip in a pleasure boat across the bay when he (or she) heard screams and saw a young swimmer in difficulties. He (or she) jumped overboard and swam with her back to the boat. The girl, Susie Roberts, was taken to hospital but is now fully recovered.

BOMB SCARE

A bomb was found in a ladies' fashion shop in Plymouth today. Police managed to defuse the bomb before it exploded. The Animal Freedom Fighters claimed responsibility. The shop sold fur coats.

---

* write the name of a suitable student here

Letters

Dear Letterdesk,

  I thought you would like to know about my son Timothy who has just made a trip round the world on a bicycle. He left England two years ago and travelled through Europe and Asia to Shanghai in China, where he took a boat to San Francisco, and cycled right across the USA before coming home. We thought maybe you would like to interview him on your programme.

> Yours sincerely
> Mavis Leadbetter (Mrs)

Dear Letterdesk,

  The council's plans for the new by-pass show it passing right through an area of beautiful woodland. Our family, and many other families too, often go there for weekend walks and picnics. What a shame to destroy this tranquil countryside with a noisy road and spoil the innocent pleasure of hundreds of local residents.

> Yours sincerely
> Mary Drummond

Dear Letterdesk,

  Many of your viewers write in to say what a good idea the new by-pass is and what a great improvement it will be. But spare a thought for the poor shopkeepers! Now that most cars will go along the by-pass instead of through the town, we will lose many of our customers!

> Yours
> Jim Thompson (butcher)

Dear Letterdesk,
   I thought you would like to know about my uncle Samuel Jarvis who is 100 years old today, and is the oldest resident of this town. I thought you might like to interview him on your programme. He has lots of very interesting memories.
                    Yours truly
                    Ada Myers (Miss)
P.S. He is a bit deaf so you will have to speak up.

Dear Letterdesk,
   I think you should interview my aunt on your programme. She collects tea cups. She has over 1,000 of them and knows a story about every one. Most of them belonged to famous people.
                    From
                    Anna (age 9)

Dear Letterdesk,
        I'm sure I'm not the only person in this town who is shocked and disgusted by foreign students. Our town is full of foreigners of all kinds. The young ones are the worst. They've got no manners, they shout all the time, they never queue for buses and they talk about me in foreign languages. They've all got long hair, they look dirty and they wear filthy clothes.
        Why don't they all go back where they come from?
                    Yours faithfully
                    George Atkins

Dear Letterdesk

I am foreigner who study English in university. I hope you don't mind my telling opinion about this town.

In my opinion this town is too bored. And there are so many old people dogs. There is too quiet in evenings, no happening. Only we can go to disco where too much loud music and without food so we can't speaking. Also is very expensive.

I'm sorry to say it also that English people are not friendly to us and ~~imporight~~ impolite

If you want that people come here please to make changes.

Sincerely yours,

Kyoko Ho

Memo
Correct the English on this one!
Producer

Dear Letterdesk,

I know a lot of people don't like foreign students but I don't agree!

I must tell you what happened to me the other day. I was crossing Union street with my shopping yesterday when my shopping basket broke. Well! Everything was lying in the middle of the road. I'm not very quick on my feet as I'm 83 and I cant bend because I've got a wooden leg. But luckily a group of foreign students saw me. They picked up my shopping, repaired my basket and carried it all home for me! One of the young men helped me home, it made me feel like a young girl again!

They were so sweet and friendly. I invited them in for a cup of tea. I don't think our English young people are nearly as nice.

Please tell your listeners!

Yours sincerely

Ida Martin (Mrs.)

> Dear Letterdesk Presenter,
>   I must tell you how I feel about you! I can't sleep, I can't eat, I think about you all the time! I walk around in a dream all the time. People are beginning to talk about me at work. Please let me meet you sometime!
>
> I am tall with blond hair. People tell me I am good-looking especially my eyes which are deep blue-grey.
>
> If you can meet me, please use the words 'Lovely to be with you again' instead of 'Hallo and good evening' when you introduce the programme. Then I will meet you outside the studio after the programme.
>
> You must say it! I can't live without you!
>   Yours in anticipation, forever,
>   Alex Hunter

Acknowledgement

I first got the idea for making a TV programme from using the simulation 'Radio Covingham'.

11.4 Travel posters

LEVEL

Elementary and above

TIME

One lesson

MATERIALS

Large sheet of paper for each group, coloured pens

PROCEDURE

1 You can introduce this activity with some reading material from travel brochures if you like, to give the students an example of the type of writing used in travel literature and to provide them with some typical adjectives.

2 Put the students in groups, ensuring that each group contains at least two different nationalities. If your students are monolingual but come from different towns, put them in groups where at least two towns are represented.

3 Give out pens and paper and tell the students that their task is to design a travel poster advertising a country (town). *But* this must not be the country (town) of any one person in the group but a made-up place consisting of the best features of every place

represented in the group. For example, a group advert made by Italian, Japanese, and Moroccan students might contain references to delicious spaghetti, exotic bazaars, ornate temples, and so on. Groups should make up a name for their place.

4 When the posters are finished, display them around the classroom. Students can then walk around and decide which places to visit.

11.5 Group scrapbook

LEVEL

Elementary and above

TIME

15 minutes once a week

MATERIALS

Large (A3) pieces of paper

PREPARATION

This is a cumulative group scrapbook that will provide a record of the group's experiences over the term. If you have a photocopier that reduces, you or they can make a small-scale copy for every student as a souvenir. Set aside a time every week for this activity. Monday or Friday are probably good times.

Think of a topic or angle for every week, for example (for students in Britain):

Week 1: First impressions of Britain
Week 2: Our class
Week 3: Other countries
Week 4: Learning English
Week 5: At the weekend . . .
Week 6: Friends
Week 7: Things to do in . . .
Week 8: Places to visit
Week 9: Misunderstandings
Week 10: Family life in Britain
Week 11: Social customs
Week 12: My best memories

For students studying in their own countries, it is best if you make your own list depending on their ages and interests.

PROCEDURE

1 Give the students the topic, and talk around it a little with them.

2 Then ask them to write on it for fifteen minutes. They may write whatever comes into their head.

3 Collect up the scripts.

4 Edit them at home, choosing the best sections, and write or type them out, correcting any mistakes.

5 Stick them onto the large piece of paper to make an attractive display and pin it up on the classroom wall for that week.

REMARKS

The students can also add other items such as postcards, pictures from magazines, photos, dried flowers, etc. to illustrate the themes if they wish.

12 Bringing it together: pyramid discussions, feedback techniques, and summaries

In many ways pairwork or small group work can be a destructive activity. I do not mean to deny the obvious benefits of pairwork. But one must balance against the advantages the fact that pairwork is in essence divisive in that it fragments the class. Many pairwork activities also tend to focus on disagreement and conflict of opinions, while many are open-ended, with no real goal or satisfying conclusion. This means that you have some powerful hidden factors working against cohesion and harmony in your classroom.

Students sometimes complain about pair- or groupwork. A common tendency among teachers is to see this kind of complaint as conservatism, a refusal to open up to ways of working that might be different from the traditions the students are used to, or a kind of selfishness where they don't believe they can learn anything from another student, but want the teacher's undivided attention. But maybe these students are also expressing or trying to rationalize a certain unsatisfied feeling that pairwork seems to produce.

I am not, of course, suggesting that we abandon pairwork. Clearly, it has a vital function. I am suggesting that we should think carefully about how we use it, and particularly about how we can use it without leading to a sense of fragmentation, conflict, or purposelessness. In Chapter 4, 'Bridging gaps', I suggested pair- and groupwork activities which bring people together rather than focusing on differences. In Chapter 11, 'Group achievements', I suggested group activities with a definite goal or end-product. Here I would like to look at some ways of rounding pairwork off, of making it less inconclusive and open-ended, and bringing it to a definite conclusion, involving the whole class. This section focuses less on 'one-off' activities than on broadly generalizable techniques that can be used with many pair or group activities. The techniques all have the common aim of returning the pair to the whole group, and in doing so, getting them to reflect on what went on in the pair or small group activity and present that activity in a more concrete or permanent form to the whole class.

12.1 Pyramid discussions

This technique brings a discussion in gradual stages from pairwork to a whole-class format.

1 Start the discussion with students in pairs, then group pairs into fours, then fours into eights.

2 At each stage participants should relay to each other what was said in the previous stage and then continue the discussion, which should increase in depth and complexity as each new facet is added. It is best to give a shortish time-limit for each stage, so that students do not completely exhaust all their ideas at the beginning, and feel they are tired of the topic by the time the discussion reaches the whole-class stage.

3 At this stage you can pull it together, by asking one student from each group to report on what was said, before throwing the discussion open to the whole class.

12.2 Reporting back

1 Proceed as for 'Pyramid discussions' as far as the 'fours' stage.

2 At this stage, give the group as much time as it needs to discuss issues fully.

3 When they have finished, give them a little time as a group to go back over the discussion and to recollect what was said. They may make notes at this stage.

4 Then ask one person from each group to act as spokesperson and to summarize for the class what was said in their group.

Instead of a spokesperson reporting verbally, a 'group scribe' could write a summary of the discussion and display it for the rest of the class to read. See 14.3.

12.3 Poster presentations

1 At the end of a discussion, give each group a poster-size piece of paper, coloured pens, coloured paper, scissors, and glue, and ask them to prepare a poster summary of the opinions expressed in their discussion. You may need to give some ideas for layout: for example, if opinions were divided into two camps, they could show this graphically by dividing the poster in half, or by using two different colours for the different opinions, or different coloured speech bubbles to summarize what different group members said.

2 Pin the posters round the room when everyone has finished, and finish off the lesson by letting everyone walk around and read them.

12.4 Postbag

PROCEDURE

1 Finish off a role play by asking each member of the group to write a letter to a friend, in character, expressing their views and describing the incident the group have just played out.

2 Collect up the letters and act as 'postman', redistributing letters across the class. Try to ensure that letters are received by a student who played a different role from the writer of the letter.

3 Ask the recipients to imagine they are a sympathetic friend and to write a reply.

4 Pin letters and replies up around the room and ask students to walk round and read them.

12.5 Instant opinion poll

PROCEDURE

1 This activity can be used to round off a pairwork discussion activity of the values clarification type, where students are asked to say whether they agree or disagree with certain statements and how strongly they feel about them. Assign one of the statements to each student or pair, and give them the task of finding how many students in the class agreed strongly, felt neutral, or disagreed strongly.

2 Get them to present their findings as a graph or pie chart on a small piece of paper.

3 Arrange and glue these onto a poster-size piece of paper and pin this up for students to read and comment on.

12.6 Storybook

PROCEDURE

1 If the group or pair activity centred around the telling of personal anecdotes, get students to write these up at the end of the group activity.

2 Collect them in, and type them up, correcting errors as you go, to make a group storybook. Alternatively, record the anecdotes on tape for students to listen to in class, or in their own time.

12.7 Amazing facts

1 At the end of a group or pair discussion, ask each group or pair to select the two or three most surprising things that came out in the discussion, for example: 'Roberto is afraid of spiders!' or 'None of us were ever slapped when we were children!' or 'Susanna thinks every house will have a video telephone by the year 2000!'

2 Ask them to write these with coloured pens on strips of paper.

3 Prepare a poster headed 'Amazing Facts' and glue the strips on to the poster to make an attractive and eye-catching display. Pin the poster on the wall.

13 That patriotic class feeling: inter-class activities and competitions

A group will have a stronger sense of itself if it can define itself in contrast to another group. This is very obviously a dangerous area, as this is the kind of emotion that can lead to nationalism, racism, and wars. However, there are perfectly healthy situations where two groups compete against each other: sports teams, parliamentary parties in a democracy, families in TV quiz shows, or Welsh choirs at an eisteddfod. I think that provided the activity is kept light-hearted and fun, inter-class activities and games where one class competes with or interacts with another can help group cohesion by giving the class a sense of themselves as a group. Paradoxically, such activities can at the same time provide a bit of fresh air and a release from the group, in the shape of new people to talk to and new ideas.

The activities suggested here range from the fairly serious ('Inter-class debate') to the totally frivolous ('Silly sports') and have been chosen to include examples of different kinds of activity such as quizzes, drama, role play, and games.

13.1 Inter-class debate

LEVEL

Intermediate and above

TIME

Two lessons on consecutive days

PROCEDURE

1 Choose a debate topic in consultation with your students and the teacher and students of the other class involved.

2 Decide which class is going to support the motion and which is going to oppose it.

3 Involve your whole class in writing the speeches for the proposer and seconder, as follows. Begin by giving each student a pile of small pieces of paper. Give them a time-limit to write down all their ideas on the subject, one idea per piece of paper. Get them to write as quickly as possible.

4 Put them in pairs and get them to share ideas and write more if they can.

5 Then ask for ideas from the whole class. Note these down on the board or OHP as they say them.

6 Then work on a strategy for the debate with the class. Get them to put the ideas in three groups: most important, secondary, and interesting additions. Let them decide which should go in the main speech, which should go in the seconder's speech, and which could be kept in reserve for comments from the floor. (This can lead to a very interesting discussion on tactics!)

7 Then write the two speeches with the class (they do not have to be very long), drafting and re-drafting, deciding in what order the points should be made and how to express them most forcefully. An OHP is better than a blackboard at this point, and if you have a small class in a hi-tech establishment, a word-processor would be ideal.

8 Finally, let the class decide which speakers should represent them. The speakers have extra homework that night: they have to reduce their speeches to note form and practise speaking from the notes.

9 The next day, assemble the two classes, appoint a student as chair, and have the debate.

REMARKS

I find this a more satisfactory format for a debate than doing it as a simple class activity. The preparation stage allows the whole class to get involved in the arguments and in writing the speeches, and so when the time for the actual debate arrives they have some personal investment in the proceedings.

13.2 Package tours

LEVEL

Intermediate and above

TIME

One lesson

PREPARATION

Prepare the activity in advance with a teacher from another group.

PROCEDURE

1 Ask your class to imagine they are all inhabitants of an imaginary country. Build up a profile of the country with them by asking questions and noting down the answers on the board or OHP. Facts you should establish are:

– Where is the country?
– Is it an island or part of a land mass?
– What is the climate like?

– What is the landscape like?
– What is the vegetation?
– What are the main geographical areas?
– What are the people like?
– What are the main industries and crops?
– What is its political system?
– What are the main towns?
– What is it famous for?

The rule is that as soon as a student volunteers any information, it is written down and becomes fact! It will help to draw a map of the country as you go along.

2 When you have established these basic facts, divide the students into groups corresponding to geographical areas.

3 Tell them they can now invent more details about their area, provided that they do not contradict what has already been established by the class.

4 When they have had some time to do this, tell them that there are some package tours coming to the country. The tourists will visit all the different areas, and the inhabitants should be ready to receive them and tell them about the history, customs, and tourist attractions of their area.

5 Invite the other class in, dividing them up into three or four package tours who will follow different routes round the 'country'. The 'natives' in each area should welcome them, show them the sights, and tell them all about their area.

6 When the tour is over, your class can become package tourists in the class's 'country'. (If you prefer, you can send half a class at a time to be tourists, while the other half remain as 'hosts'.)

13.3 Inter-class quiz league

LEVEL	**All**
TIME	**20–30 minutes**
MATERIALS	**Master list of quiz questions, watch, bell**
PREPARATION	Prepare a list of quiz questions with a colleague or colleagues. These can be general knowledge questions or questions that practise a particular structure, such as superlatives ('Which is the longest river in the world?'), simple past ('Who invented the steam engine?'), or passives ('Where is copper produced?'), or which test students' knowledge of Britain, America, the town they are in, or each others' cultures.

PROCEDURE

1 Get each class to select a quiz team of four or five people.

2 Seat these two teams at the front of the room with the Question Master (teacher or student) seated between them. The Question Master should have a watch and a bell.

3 Questions should be asked alternately of each team. If the team can answer within the time-limit, they get a point. If not, the Question Master should ring the bell and throw the question open to the floor. The first person to answer gets a point for the appropriate team. The team with the most points is the winner.

REMARKS

This can be a one-off event, related to syllabus content, or a recreational activity. It is possible to organize a quiz league, with different teams playing against each other to reach the final. In this case it is essential to ask a colleague with good general knowledge to write the questions!

13.4 Silly sports

LEVEL

All

TIME

A sunny afternoon

MATERIALS

Rope, bicycles, trays with plastic bottles and cups, etc., old clothes, eggs, spoons, sacks, scarves for each team, whistle, prizes

PREPARATION

This a whole-school activity with class teams competing against each other. Book a sports field. Decide which events you want to include. (Some suggestions are given below.) Assemble the necessary props. Circulate a copy of the programme round the classes and get volunteers to sign up for the events. Work out the order of events, and how teams are going to play against each other in rounds leading to a final for each event. Choose a colleague with a loud voice to announce events and winners. If your class really want to enter into the spirit of it and impart an American flavour to the afternoon, they can make banners and devise songs.

PROCEDURE

On the afternoon, take all the students to the sports field and organize the sports day.

Suggestions for events
Dressing-up relay: Teams of four from each class, two at each end of the track as for a traditional relay. Place two piles of clothing in the middle of the track. When the whistle is blown, the first runners should race to the clothes, put them on, and continue to the end of the track, where they should undress and hand the

clothes to the next runner who must put them on before running, and so on until all four team members have dressed, undressed, and run the race.

Egg and spoon: One competitor from each class. Give each competitor a spoon and hard-boiled egg. The first to reach the end of the track with the egg still on the spoon is the winner. No holding on allowed.

Slow bicycle race: One competitor from each class. The person who can ride a bike most *slowly* from one end of the track to the other is the winner.

Waiters' relay: Teams of four from each class, two at each end of the track as for a traditional relay. Give the first runner in each team a tray with plastic bottles and cups. They should run to the other end of the track balancing the tray and bottles on one hand, hand over the tray to the next team-member, and so on. The first team to finish with a full tray is the winner.

Sack race: One competitor from each class. Competitors get into sacks, and jump their way from one end of the track to the other.

Three-legged race: Teams of two from each class. Teams tie their ankles together with a scarf or large handkerchief, and run with three legs from one end of the track to the other.

Wheelbarrow race: Teams of two from each class. One of each pair crouches down on the ground, the other picks up their ankles, and they run together on hands and feet to the end of the track.

Tug-of-war: Each whole class acts as a team. One class takes each end of the rope, and pulls. The strongest class wins.

REMARKS

This makes a nice silly afternoon, and provides a very relaxing break in a term. It is obviously better held in spring, summer, or early autumn. The frivolity of the races ensures that the whole event is light-hearted and not seriously competitive.

13.5 Sketches

LEVEL

All (though for beginners you will have to simplify the language, and probably rely more on demonstration than comprehension)

TIME

Preparation time: one or two lessons
Acting time: 45 minutes

MATERIALS

Clothes for dressing up, props as necessary

1 Divide the class into three groups and give each a written summary of the sketch.

2 Let them work it out themselves with guidance from you.

3 Then they present their mime to the other groups.

4 More work will now be needed to make the sketches slick and presentable, and you will have to rehearse them several times to get good co-ordination and timing.

5 When the sketches are as good as possible, present them to another class or classes one evening or lunch hour.

Present the sketches firstly as a listening exercise:
Read out the directions, and pause, either designating a student to come forward and take the role, or waiting for someone to take the initiative and volunteer. A good way of designating students you think would be suitable for the roles is to describe them as you read the sketch description, for example: 'A young man was standing at a bus stop. He was wearing a blue-striped T-shirt and grey jeans'. You should make sure that every student has a part in at least one sketch.

The Tramp
Put four or five chairs together in a line. This is a park bench. An old tramp in a filthy overcoat is asleep on the bench, lying full-length with a newspaper over his face and snoring. A smartly dressed businessman comes into the park. He is carrying a newspaper and his sandwiches. He sees the bench and goes over to sit on the end, near the tramp's feet. The tramp grunts and moves his legs. The businessman begins to read his paper and eat his sandwiches. Now a lady carrying two heavy shopping bags comes into the park. She is tired and is looking for somewhere to sit down. She comes over to the bench. The businessman taps the tramp on the shoulder and gestures to him to make room. He curls up more tightly and the lady sits down with a sigh of relief. Next, a woman with a little girl comes into the park. The little girl is sucking a lollipop. They come over to sit on the bench. Now the tramp has to sit up. He isn't very pleased about this. The last people to come and sit on the bench are a boy and his girlfriend. They hold hands and gaze into each others' eyes. The tramp is not happy. Suddenly, he gets a good idea! He begins to scratch, first his head, then his arms, then his legs ... first slowly, then more urgently. Gradually, the businessman sitting next to him begins to scratch, then the lady with the shopping, then the woman and child, then the couple. They scratch slowly at first, then more and more furiously, until everyone on the bench is scratching. Suddenly, something occurs to them. They stop, look at the tramp, look at each other, and then, as one person, get up and run away! The tramp smiles happily, and stretches out on the bench again.

Chewing Gum
A bus stop. A bench near it. A young man comes along, looks at his watch, and leans back against the stop. He takes out a stick of gum, unwraps it, and begins to chew. He walks up and down while waiting. Suddenly, he sees a friend passing in a car, waves, starts off, then remembers the gum, takes it out and sticks it on the bus-stop, then rushes off. A young woman comes along next, looks at her watch, then leans back against the bus stop. Her head is exactly where the young man stuck the gum, but she doesn't notice. She sees her bus coming, starts forward to hail it, and gets an unpleasant surprise. She sorts out the sticky gum from her hair and throws it down on the pavement in disgust, boards her bus, goes off. Along comes a young man in a hurry. Running along, he steps on the gum and gets stuck, picks his foot up, removes the gum, looks around and sees the bench, sticks it on the bench, runs on. An old lady comes to the stop, looks around, sees the bench, and sits down thankfully, right on the gum. When her bus comes, she struggles up, finds she is glued to the bench, removes the gum from her skirt, looks around for somewhere to put it, and sticks it to the bus stop. Re-enter the young man, whistling a tune. He stops by the bus stop, looks at his watch, then feels in his top pocket for a stick of gum. It isn't there. He looks around and sees his gum, where he left it on the bus stop. Light dawns on his face, he detaches the gum, and goes off chewing . . .

Flasher
A cinema queue builds up: first a young man, listening to a Walkman; a young couple, arm in arm; a woman with a small child; an old lady; two friends; an old man; a young woman in a tight skirt; two more friends who see their two friends ahead of them in the queue and go up to join them; someone with heavy shopping; and finally, an old tramp in a dirty old man's mac. He tries to jump the queue. The queuers are very annoyed and gesticulate at him, pointing at the back of the queue where he should be. He tries to push into the queue at several places, with no success. Finally, he joins the back of the queue, looking rather unhappy. Then he gets an idea. With his back to the audience, but facing the queue, he moves in front of them and opens his mac. Startled, they all look in his direction, give a loud scream, and run off as fast as they can. Happily, the tramp moves to the front of the queue. He smiles at the audience, then turns and opens his mac. Pinned in the appropriate place is a photo. (Photos we have used in the past have been: a picture of the Head of Department, Margaret Thatcher, Prince Charles, and a copy of a Cambridge FCE exam paper.)

REMARKS

Two things are very important in these sketches: good timing, and clear differentiation of the individual characters on the bench, at the bus-stop, and in the queue. They should all have a prop of some sort indicating character and age, and have something to do while in the queue or sitting on the bench. I have given rough outlines, but this is something that should be developed as the rehearsals progress. As far as timing is concerned, you will have to work on this by trial and error, deciding how timing can best contribute to the comedy. It is nice to have background music, as in an old silent film. We used Charlie Chaplin music: this gives a nice rhythm to the mimes.

Acknowledgement
These sketches have been part of the folk tradition at our college for a long time. I first learned them from Tom Hunter. Where he learned them is shrouded in the mists of time...

14 Ensuring participation

A frequent problem in groups is that not all members participate equally in discussions. Sometimes a dominant member or members will take over a discussion completely, while shyer students are unable to get a word in edgeways; sometimes the problem is one of 'student passengers', as one teacher put it, who make no contribution to class activities.

It is difficult to deal with both types of student. The dominant members may be forceful or somewhat aggressive people, but often they are simply lively, enthusiastic, talkative students who contribute a great deal to the class, and it is hard to encourage the others to talk more, and them to talk a bit less, without dampening their enthusiasm. Sometimes they are not aware of the problem and thus activities designed to heighten their awareness of the imbalance in group participation may help to alleviate it. Students who make little contribution to discussions may be shy or quiet people in their own language. It is hard suddenly to be required to change your habits, and feelings of inadequacy about language ability may make this doubly hard (although for some shy students, the act of speaking another language is a kind of liberation). Activities that give such students something to say, rather than those which require invention, and activities which make turn-taking in a discussion into a kind of game rather than a real-life decision, may help with this problem.

This section suggests techniques that can be used during group discussions or speaking activities to make students more aware of the problems, and to create a better balance in discussions.

14.1 Interaction mapping

LEVEL

All

TIME

One lesson

PROCEDURE

This technique can be used during any discussion activity.

1 For each discussion group, appoint one 'observer'.

2 Tell the group that the observer is to act as secretary and will not play an active part in the discussion but will take notes of points raised.

3 Get each observer to write a diagram of the people in the group, for example:

4 Ask them simply to draw a continuous line on the paper linking the participants in the discussion in the order in which they speak. The finished diagram might look something like this:

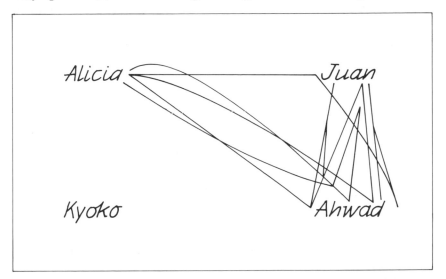

Ask the observer to sit a little apart from the group so that they do not get distracted.

5 When the discussion is over, ask the observers to show their diagram to the group, and to talk about it together: did everyone participate in the discussion? Was there equal participation? How could they get the balance better in their group?

VARIATION

You can follow this exercise with a similar one, but one where all group members are conscious of the mapping of the interactions during the discussion.

1 Give each group a ball of string.

2 The person who opens the discussion should hold one end of the string, and pass the ball on to the next person to speak, and so on. The resultant web of string will be a record of who has participated in the discussion. The difference is that as the students are aware of the activity, they can influence it, either by participating more fully, or by saying less, and bringing other people in.

14.2 Catching the question

LEVEL	**All**
TIME	**Up to one lesson**
MATERIALS	**Ball for each group**
PROCEDURE	1 Provide each discussion group with a ball. Give it to one member of the group, who must start off the discussion.
	2 When this speaker has finished, he or she should throw the ball to another member of the group, who should be the next to speak, and so on.

14.3 Group scribes

LEVEL	**Post-elementary and above**
TIME	**Up to one lesson**
MATERIALS	**Pen and paper for one member of each group**
PROCEDURE	1 Appoint a 'scribe' for each group, whose job is to take notes on what is said in the discussion. The scribe should not participate in the discussion, but keep a record of points raised by the others in the group.
	2 At the end ask the scribe from each group to report back, giving an oral summary of what was said in the group.
REMARKS	This is a good role for either a dominant or a tongue-tied group member. A dominant group member can thus be kept out of the discussion while the others have their say, but still has a role at the end. It is a good way of getting a really tongue-tied member to speak, providing something ready-made to say.

14.4 Over to you

LEVEL

Post-elementary and above

TIME

Up to one lesson

PREPARATION

Prepare a set of cards for each group: each set of cards should consist of the names of the people in that group, repeated three or four times.

PROCEDURE

1 Pre-teach turn-taking vocabulary with phrases such as 'What do you think about this?' and 'What's your opinion?'

2 Give each group their pile of cards and ask them to deal them out equally to all players.

3 Ask them to begin the discussion. When the first person has finished speaking, they should select a card from their hand and lay it on the table, asking the person whose name is on the card for their opinions on the subject.

4 As each person finishes speaking, they should take a card from their hand and invite the next player's opinions on the subject. If you prefer, the cards can be left face down in a pile on the table instead of being dealt out. They can then be turned up one at a time as each player finishes speaking. If they turn up a card with their own name on it, they should put it at the bottom of the pile and take another card.

14.5 Passing the buck

LEVEL

Post-elementary and above

TIME

Up to one lesson

MATERIALS

Set of cards for each group

PREPARATION

Make one copy of the first card for each group, and enough copies of the others for each group member to have several cards.

PROCEDURE

1 Give each group a set of cards.

2 Ask the group members to deal them out equally to all members.

3 The student with the 'Begin the discussion' card, should begin, then the others take turns according to the instructions on the card in their hands. As they use a card, they throw it away.

4 The discussion ends when one group member has got rid of all their cards.

CARDS

Start the discussion off. When you have said something about the subject, ask the student on your right for his or her opinion.	If someone asks you for your opinion, say what you think and then ask the person opposite you what they think.
If someone asks you for your opinion, say what you think and then ask the player on your left if they agree with you.	If someone asks you for your opinion, say what you think and then ask the person opposite you how they feel about the subject.

REMARKS

These last two activities, like the ball game, make the act of turn-taking in a discussion into a game. A game takes place in its own self-enclosed reality, distinct from real life. It may therefore be less threatening to shy students: the fact that turn-taking is determined by cards or a ball means that the act of taking part in the discussion is governed by chance, not by your own decision. Having the courage to take the decision to join in a heated discussion is probably what shy students find most difficult.

15 Learning to listen

One problem mentioned by many teachers in their replies to our survey was that students are often bad at listening to one another. There could be many overlapping causes for this problem: students could find one another boring; they could be seeing a speaking activity purely as an activity that practises their speaking, without realizing that in order to speak effectively and with confidence a sympathetic audience is the first requirement; they may not find listening to a non-native speaker very productive in terms of their own language learning; they may be so busy thinking out what they're going to say next that they have no time to listen to their partner; or they could just be exhibiting that very natural human tendency to be more interested in one's own preoccupations than in anyone else's. All these reasons have one thing in common, that students are viewing language learning as a narrowly individual affair. They cannot look beyond their own personal goals to the fact that communication is always reciprocal in nature. People talk more confidently and fluently if their interlocutor is giving their full attention, and in turn will respond more directly and appropriately if they have listened to, and are basing their reply on, what their partner has said, and so on.

The exercises in this section aim to help students become aware of the need to listen to each other, and to create situations where they have to listen closely to the other person. They are generalizable techniques which can be used in conjunction with any pair or group speaking activity.

15.1 Speaking to a brick wall

LEVEL   Post-elementary and above

TIME   15 minutes

MATERIALS   Role cards for each pair (see below)

PROCEDURE   1 Ask students to work with a partner for this exercise.

2 Give out the first set of paired role cards and ask them to follow the instructions on the cards.

3 Then give out the second set of role cards, reversing the roles this time, so each student has the experience of 'speaking to a brick wall'.

4 Then ask them in pairs to discuss how they felt about the experience and how it affected their fluency.

5 Ask pairs to give feedback on how they felt to the whole class.

ROLE CARDS

A

You have a problem. You think you are about to lose your job. You heard yesterday that half the employees in your company are to lose their jobs. No one knows exactly who it will be, but everyone is very anxious. It's creating a bad atmosphere. You don't know what to do: it's hard to find a similar job in this area and you don't really want to move.

B

A will tell you about a problem. You are not interested. Look out of the window, clean your nails, yawn if you like, but don't pay any attention. Don't look at A while he/she is talking. When A has finished, talk about yourself: say something like 'When's the break?', or 'I could do with a coffee', or 'I saw a really good film on TV last night'. Don't say anything about A's problem.

A

You have a problem. There's a really bad atmosphere in your flat. No-one is getting on any more. Toni is really lazy, never does any cleaning, never even does the washing-up. Everyone moans about it, but no one says anything to Toni. Alex comes back with friends at about three every morning and makes an awful noise, playing records and talking loudly. The rest of you have to get up early! And Sam is just terribly bad-tempered all the time and shouts at people over the slightest little thing. You don't know what to do!

B

A will tell you about a problem. You are not interested. Look out of the window, clean your nails, yawn if you like, but don't pay attention. Don't look at A while he/she is talking. When A has finished, talk about yourself: say something like 'When's the break?', or 'I could do with a coffee', or 'I saw a really good film on TV last night'. Don't say anything about A's problem.

REMARKS

This activity should be followed by 15.2.

Photocopiable © Oxford University Press

15.2 Tea and sympathy

LEVEL

Post-elementary and above

TIME

15 minutes

MATERIALS

A's role cards from 15.1, B's role card as below for each pair

PREPARATION

Copy role cards for each pair.

PROCEDURE

1 Students should work with the same partner as for the last exercise.

2 Ask them to repeat the role play, keeping the same roles as they had in the previous exercise, but this time change B's role card, substituting the one printed below.

3 When they have finished, ask them to discuss their experiences again: How did they feel this time? Was it easier to talk? Did their fluency improve? Did they find more to say?

ROLE CARD

B

A is a good friend of yours. He/she looks terribly upset, and you are sure he/she has a problem. Ask what's the matter, and if he/she wants to talk about the problem. While he/she is talking, listen sympathetically. Ask questions. If you are not quite sure about some details, ask about them. Ask how A feels and what he/she is going to do. Offer advice. Try to be a really good listener!

15.3 Listeners

LEVEL

Post-elementary and above

TIME

15 minutes

MATERIALS

One copy of the questionnaire for each student (or write it on the blackboard or OHP)

PREPARATION

Make copies as necessary.

PROCEDURE

1 Ask students to think about situations in their lives where they have listened to people or where people have listened to them.

2 Give out one questionnaire to each student and ask them to think about the questions on it.

3 When they are ready, ask them to discuss their answers with a partner.

4 Finally, ask each pair to tell the class the most interesting thing that came out of their discussion.

QUESTIONNAIRE

LISTENERS

Try to think of all the situations in your life where you have been a listener (to teachers at school, to a parent telling you off, to a friend with a problem...)

Who do you enjoy listening to? Who do you dislike listening to? Why?

Who listens to you? Are any of them the same people as in the first question?

Who do you enjoy talking to?

Who is a good listener? Are these the same people as in the previous question?

What is a good listener? What do they do to make you feel happy about talking to them?

15.4 Bamboo telegraph

LEVEL

All

TIME

15 minutes (at the end of a pairwork discussion)

PROCEDURE

1 At the end of a pairwork activity, ask students to change partners.

2 Ask them to summarize to their new partner what their first partner said.

3 Then ask the new partner to relay the summary to the whole class. The person whose views are being reported has the right to object if that wasn't exactly what they said!

VARIATION

1 Organize the activity as above, but at stage 2 ask students not merely to report their first partners' views, but to present them as if they are their partner, in other words to put themselves in their partner's place.

2 At stage 3 ask the second partners to repeat the process, that is, to report back to the class the views they have just heard, again in the first person, as if those opinions are their own.

Photocopiable © Oxford University Press

REMARKS

If you reseat students between the first and second phases, you can make this into a game: students put up their hands when they identify 'themselves' speaking!

15.5 Body language and showing interest

LEVEL

Lower-intermediate and above

TIME

5–10 minutes

MATERIALS

One set of role cards for each pair of students

PROCEDURE

1 Divide the class into pairs and give out the role cards. Explain that in each pair there is one 'listener' and one 'storyteller' and that they should follow the instructions on their cards as carefully as possible.

2 Allow a couple of minutes for the storyteller to think of an anecdote while the listeners ask you about words like 'fidget' and 'eye contact'.

3 When they have finished, ask the storytellers how they felt when telling the story. Did they have the listeners' attention? Did they feel encouraged to go on? What did the listener do to make them feel they were being listened to?

4 Ask them to exchange cards and reverse roles.

ROLE CARDS

Listener

Show that you are listening carefully to your partner. Don't say anything, but use 'body language':

– make eye contact

– don't fidget or let your attention wander

– encourage the speaker by nodding and smiling occasionally.

Storyteller

Tell your partner about one of the following things:

– describe your family

– describe something that happened to you when you were a child

– describe something that happened to you last week.

REMARKS

This activity is one of a sequence and is linked to the variations: you can either do them all in one lesson, or as 'warmers' to introduce speaking skills lessons.

VARIATION 1

Follow the same procedure as above, but use the role cards below to show interest verbally.

ROLE CARDS

Listener

Your partner will tell you a short anecdote. Listen carefully. Show you are interested and encourage your partner to continue by using phrases like:
– Go on!
– What happened next?
– So what did you do?
– Really?
– How did you feel then?
Try to be as natural as possible.

Storyteller

Tell a short anecdote, for instance:

– about something that happened to you on holiday
– something funny that happened to you or one of your family.

Or you can invent something if you prefer:

– an accident you were involved in
– a crime you witnessed.

VARIATION 2

Follow the same procedure as above, but use the role cards below.

ROLE CARDS

Listener

Listen to your partner who will try to explain how he/she feels about something that happened the other day. The problem is, he/she is a bit confused about his/her feelings, so listen carefully while he/she tries to describe them to you and help him/her by asking questions like:
Do you mean that...?
Are you saying that...?
What do you mean by...?
How did you feel about that...?
So now you feel...?

> **Storyteller**
>
> Last week a friend of yours asked to borrow some money. You didn't really want to lend him the money, but you did. That was six weeks ago. He still hasn't paid you back. You saw him yesterday and he didn't mention it. Now you learn he's going on holiday next week. You are very confused and don't really know how you feel about the situation. Describe what happened to your partner, trying to explain your feelings about your friend.

VARIATION 3

Follow the same procedure as above, but use the role cards below.

ROLE CARDS

> **Listener**
>
> Your partner will tell you something about his/her feelings. To your surprise he/she is describing exactly how you feel about the subject too! Join in and agree with her. You can use phrases like:
> – Oh yes!
> – Me too!
> – I feel just the same!
> – I know just how you feel.
> – I know what you mean.
> – That's how I feel too.

> **Storyteller**
>
> Tell your partner how you feel about speaking English. Say
> – whether you think your English is good or bad
> – when you feel shy about speaking English
> – when you feel good about speaking English
> – how you feel when you don't understand what someone is saying.

REMARKS

'Reporting back' (12.2) can also be used as a good listening exercise. If it is used following pairwork, students report back on what their partner said.

16 A sense of direction: setting, assessing, and resetting goals

It is fundamental to the successful working of a group to have a sense of direction and a common purpose. Defining and agreeing aims is one of the hardest tasks that the group has to undertake together. It can be hard for many reasons: students may not have defined their own aims clearly to themselves; they may have only a hazy notion of what learning a language involves; they may think that the traditional grammar-translation techniques they used at school are what language learning is about; or they may have very precise and narrow aims of their own, which may conflict with others' aims or the wider aims of the group. The teacher has the difficult task not only of helping students individually to clarify their aims, but of somehow weaving all these individual wants and needs together into a coherent programme which satisfies everyone in the group. The activities in this section encourage students not only to think about their own aims and define them more clearly, but also to think in terms of group aims and strategies. They help them to decide what are group aims and what are private aims, and to think how they can co-operate with each other to achieve these aims. They encourage students to set goals for themselves and for the group, to assess at intervals whether these goals have been met, and to reset them if they were too ambitious. The activities are a continuation of the process begun in Chapters 2 and 3, 'Thinking about language' and 'Thinking about groups', and may be done in conjunction with the activities in Chapter 17, 'Coexistence and compromise'.

16.1 I'm here because...

LEVEL	**Intermediate and above** (all levels if mother tongue allowed)
TIME	**20 minutes**
MATERIALS	**Copy of the questionnaire and interpretation sheet for each student** (see below)

PROCEDURE

1 Give each student a questionnaire and ask them to fill it in.

2 Then give out the 'Interpretation sheet' and ask them to read what is written about the statements they have ticked. (They will probably read the others too!)

3 When they have finished ask them to discuss their answers with a partner.

4 Expand this into a pyramid discussion, with small groups and finally the whole class. This will help awareness of the different needs and motivations of individuals in the group and provide a basis for the negotiation of group learning priorities.

QUESTIONNAIRE

> **Tick (√) the statements that are true for you.**
>
> I'm here because...
> 1 I have to learn English. ☐
> 2 I want to learn English. ☐
> 3 I want to speak to people on holiday. ☐
> 4 I need English for my job. ☐
> 5 I have to pass an exam. ☐
> 6 I want to pass an exam. ☐
> 7 I'm going to study in English. ☐
> 8 I need to read English books or reports. ☐

INTERPRETATION SHEET

> **If you ticked (1), 'I have to learn English':**
> Think about how you learned something else successfully—riding a bike or driving a car, for example. One of the main reasons you were successful was because you *wanted* to learn. Somehow, to be successful you must really want to learn. Also see the next comment.
>
> **If you ticked (2), 'I want to learn English':**
> What do you mean? Do you want to learn to speak English like a native speaker? Think of all the non-native speaker teachers you have had. How long have they studied? Do they know English like a native speaker? Are you setting yourself a reasonable task?
>
> **If you ticked (3), 'I want to speak to people on holiday':**
> Do you mean you only want to be able to shop or buy train tickets? Or do you want to discuss philosophy? What will you need to do what you want? Can you reasonably achieve this during the course?
>
> **If you ticked (4), 'I need English for my job':**
> See the first comment. Think about exactly what you need. Do you need to answer the phone, write business letters, read instruction manuals, or talk to clients? How will this influence what you do on the course?

If you ticked (5), 'I have to pass an exam':
See the first comment. As well as thinking about essay-writing, reading comprehension, and exam techniques, think about whether you will want to use English after the exam. How will this influence what you do on the course?

If you ticked (6), 'I want to pass an exam':
See the previous comment.

If you ticked (7), 'I'm going to study in English':
Think about the skills you will need: faster extensive reading, note-taking, assignment writing, and so on. How will this influence what you want from the course?

If you ticked (8), 'I need to read English books or reports':
What will you need in order to do that? Specialized vocabulary, techniques for guessing the meaning of words, reading skills? How will this influence what you want from the course?

16.2 Visualize it

LEVEL

Post-elementary and above (all levels if mother tongue allowed)

TIME

10–15 minutes

MATERIALS

Tape of gentle music

PROCEDURE

1 Relax the students with music, and, if you like, the following relaxation technique: talking slowly and calmly with soft background music, ask students to get into the most comfortable position they can (lying down if possible) and with eyes closed, focus on different muscles, tightening them and then relaxing them: 'Tighten all the muscles in your face, go on, screw it up, now let go, feel the release . . . now tighten your neck . . . and so on. It is worth spending a little time on relaxation if the following visualization is to work properly.

2 Ask students with eyes closed to visualize some time after the course when they will have proof that they have achieved their goals, for example: they are on holiday, they hear someone talk in English in a shop, at a dinner table, on a train, they understand, they reply and are understood. Or, they are in the office, their boss gives them a report in English to summarize. They read it, understand it, write an efficient summary, and the boss smiles in appreciation, as they hand it back. Ask them to picture their own particular success story very clearly, to hear the sounds, smell the smells, and feel the feelings of pride and satisfaction.

3 Ask students in pairs or small groups to share their visualization, before moving on to another activity. (16.3, 'What do I want?', follows on well.)

16.3 What do I want?

LEVEL

Post-elementary and above (all levels if mother tongue allowed)

TIME

15–20 minutes

PROCEDURE

1 Write the following on the board and ask the students to copy and complete it for themselves:

LONG-TERM GOAL
By the end of the course I want to . . .
My first step towards this goal is . . .

SHORT-TERM GOAL
This week I will therefore . . .

2 Ask students to discuss and comment on their long- and short-term goals in groups or pairs to check that they are realistic and achievable. You may need to give help by giving examples and/or brainstorming possible weekly goals.

Possible examples of weekly goals: reading one book in English, starting and using a vocabulary notebook, finding out how the self-access centre works and making a realistic timetable to use it, writing an essay and three letters in English, and so on.

3 Open the discussion out into a whole-class discussion on which goals are common to the group as a whole, or can be accommodated into a group syllabus, and which goals are private and need self-study. (See also 17.5, 'Negotiating the timetable'.)

16.4 How I can help you, how you can help me

LEVEL

Post-elementary and above (all levels if mother tongue allowed)

TIME

10 minutes

PROCEDURE

1 Ask students to reflect a little on ways in which other students can help them to achieve their goals. Give them a little time to jot some ideas down.

2 Ask them to think about how they could help others.

3 Put students in pairs to share ideas and think of some more.

4 Then ask for ideas from the group and write them up on the board, OHP, or on a wall-poster.

REMARKS

This follows on well from the previous activity.

16.5 Have I got what I wanted?

LEVEL

Post-elementary and above (all levels if mother tongue allowed)

TIME

Variable

MATERIALS

One small notebook per student

PROCEDURE

Ask students to keep a record ('goal diary') of their progress towards their long-term goal (see 16.3), noting down what they have done each day or each week in class or on their own, and how this contributed to their goal.

VARIATION 1

At the end of lessons, ask students to spend a minute or two thinking about and discussing or noting in 'goal diaries' how the lesson helped them individually towards their long- or short-term goals.

VARIATION 2

At the same time every week (Fridays are a good time), give students time to discuss how well they feel they achieved their weekly goal. If they didn't achieve it, why not? Was it too ambitious, or did they not try hard enough? Ask them to think about the goal for next week.

REMARKS

As a teacher, you may feel rather threatened by this, but it is surprising how everyone usually manages to find something specifically relevant to them, given a little thinking time (and a positive attitude!), even if the goals of the group members are disparate.

16.6 What we've done

LEVEL

Post-elementary and above (all levels if mother tongue allowed)

TIME

10–15 minutes

MATERIALS

One copy of checklist per student (see below)

PREPARATION

Prepare a list of work covered in the past week (see checklist), and make one copy per student.

PROCEDURE

1 Give out the checklist and ask students to assess themselves.

2 Then ask them to consider their assessment in terms of their personal goals, and decide what they want to do about it. For example, if they have assessed themselves as knowing something 'Not very well', but they don't consider it important to them at this stage, they need not worry. However, if they think they

know something 'Not very well', but want to know it 'Very well' in order to achieve their goal, more class time must be negotiated, or self-study undertaken.

3 Class feedback will indicate whether more class time is justified in any area in terms of majority goals and needs, or whether certain students need guidance on specific self-study

SAMPLE CHECKLIST

Assess yourself	Not very well	OK	Very well
Reading Skimming: using titles and headlines Finding the topic sentence			
Writing Getting and organizing ideas Comparison and contrast Request letters			
Listening News broadcasts			
Speaking Giving opinions Bringing other people in			
Grammar Past perfect Past perfect continuous			
Vocabulary Word-building using un/in/mis/dis Topics: Pollution Families			

Acknowledgement
Most of the activities in this section were suggested to me by Angi Malderez.

17 Coexistence and compromise: individual wants and frustrations; group solutions

The ability to compromise is fundamental to a successful working group. If everyone in the group is only intent on getting what they want at all costs, then the group becomes an obstacle in the way of individual ambitions instead of a support system and a source of strength. Paradoxically, it is this very insistence on individual wants and ambitions that, by dividing the group into factions, makes those ambitions harder to achieve. If, for example, Faction A want traditional grammar teaching but Faction B think grammar is a waste of time and want to do as much speaking and listening as possible, then unless a compromise can be negotiated to everyone's satisfaction, the kind of uncomfortable, antagonistic situation can arise where Faction A signal their dissatisfaction by refusing to co-operate in any speaking activities, while Faction B retaliate by showing very plainly how boring they find grammar lessons. The net result can be that nobody's aims are achieved, and that everyone has a thoroughly miserable time. The tragedy is that, given a different attitude, the group would be learning perfectly well—from the activities they are less enthusiastic about as well as those they favour.

The activities in this section are discussion activities where students are placed in a situation where they have to come to an agreement which is satisfactory to all parties. Emphasis is placed on creative solutions, that is, finding imaginative ways out of the log-jam instead of reaching deadlock or a half-hearted and unsatisfactory compromise. The activities are partly affective and partly cognitive. They are affective in that, by requiring students to make compromises in imaginary situations, where they have no personal emotional involvement in the issues, they encourage them to enter into and perhaps even enjoy the business of reaching a group compromise. The cognitive aspect is the reflection phase, where students are encouraged to think about and try to understand the processes involved in making a creative compromise. The activities can be used either simply as discussion activities, or as part of a process leading up to student negotiations and decisions on the timetable and content of the course.

17.1 Ideal homes

LEVEL

Lower-intermediate and above

TIME

45 minutes

MATERIALS

Paper and pen for each group, copies of the questionnaire (see below)

PREPARATION

Copy questionnaire for each group, or write it on the board or OHP.

PROCEDURE

1 Divide the students into groups of four to six.

2 Ask them to close their eyes and imagine their perfect house. What would it be like? Big or small? How many rooms? What would the living room be like? What about the kitchen? Would there be an attic? What about the garden? Have they got any special interests or hobbies that they need special rooms or equipment for? What is the most important thing in the house for them? Give them a few minutes to visualize their house.

3 Then ask them to open their eyes and work with their group. Their task is to design a communal house that they would all like to live in. Ask them to draw a plan of the house.

4 When all the groups have finished, ask one person from each group to report back to the class as a whole, describing their house and the reasons behind its design features.

5 Then ask each group to look at their design again. Tell them their house is too expensive: they can only have half the number of rooms. Ask them to discuss what sacrifices and what compromises they would make.

6 When they have finished, give them the questionnaire and ask them to think about it in their group.

7 When they have had time to reflect and to discuss it, draw their experiences together in a whole-class discussion.

REMARKS

The questionnaire is quite searching, but in my experience the feedback is usually positive. Students seem to enjoy the second, restricted, phase of the activity as much as the first, and come up with some very ingenious solutions to ensure that everyone still gets what they want. This can make a good introduction to and analogy with the process of negotiating the timetable with the students, or to the concept of win–win negotiations in the following activities.

QUESTIONNAIRE

1 In the first phase, when you had complete freedom, how did you make the decisions about what to include in your house?

2 Did you enjoy making these decisions?

3 Did everyone get what they wanted?

4 Was there any difference in the second phase: how did you make the decisions about what to include and what to reject?

5 Did you enjoy making these decisions?

6 Did everyone get exactly what they wanted? If not, why not?

7 Did anyone have to make sacrifices? Who made the sacrifices?

8 Did they do it voluntarily? Was it fair?

9 Do you all feel happy about the house?

17.2 Win–lose and win–win negotiations

LEVEL **Lower-intermediate and above**

TIME **45 minutes**

MATERIALS **Role cards for each group** (see below)

PROCEDURE 1 Put the students into groups of three or four.

2 Give out the role cards and deal with any vocabulary problems.

3 Ask the students to discuss the problem. For groups of three leave out one card.

4 After they have been arguing for five to ten minutes or so, stop the role play. Ask them how near they are to solving the problem, if anyone is winning the argument, if anyone is losing, or if there is deadlock.

5 Then introduce the idea of 'win–win' negotiations (compromise solutions where everyone 'wins' rather than 'win–lose' showdowns where one party has to 'lose').

6 Ask them to reflect on the problem silently for five minutes, thinking of as many solutions as possible where everyone 'wins'. They should think as laterally as possible: it doesn't matter how strange or off-beat their solutions are. It may help to give each student a small pile of slips of paper. Ask them to write ideas down as fast as they come to them: one idea per slip of paper.

7 Then ask the group to pool ideas and to try to come up with an idea where no one feels they have 'lost' or been taken unfair advantage of, but which solves the dispute in a satisfactory way.

8 Ask each group to report back to the class on the solution they found at the end.

REMARKS You can follow this role play with 17.4, 'Timetabling priorities'.

ROLE CARDS **Village Green**

A
You are quite old now and you've lived in the village all your life. You like to go down to the village green in the afternoons and sit on a bench. There are a lot of other old people in the village and you all like to sit and chat. The trouble is that now the green seems to be full of kids playing football, or teenagers who roar up on motorbikes and spend their time not doing anything very much. The kids with the footballs have no consideration for anyone else—a football hit you on the head the other day. It's not a pleasant place to sit any more.

B
You like to play football after school with your mates—you're practising for the school team. You play on the village green. The only problem is that it's not really big enough and in the afternoon it gets full of boring old guys who sit around nattering on the benches which you use to mark the goals. They seem to think they own the place! They get quite cross when you start kicking the ball around. The green is for everybody!

C
There's nothing to do in the village where you live. It's really boring. You're 18, and you'd like somewhere to go with friends. You'd like a coffee bar, or a club, or something. At the moment you all hang around the village green, but it's dead boring there, always full of old people droning on about nothing, or stupid little kids playing football. The old guys keep telling you to go and do something useful instead of hanging around, and the kids get really irritated if you get in the way of their game. You wish you lived in town!

D
You're a young mum with two small toddlers. It drives you mad being cooped up in the house all day, so you like to get out with the kids. The trouble is, there's nowhere to take them. You haven't got a garden, and the village green is always full—the old men take up all the benches and the schoolkids play football—it's really dangerous with all those footballs whizzing around. It would be nice to have a play area for the little ones, with a sandpit or something.

17.3 Middlemen

LEVEL

Elementary and above

TIME

10–15 minutes per role play

MATERIALS

Role cards for each group

PROCEDURE

1 Divide the class into groups of three as far as possible.

2 Arrange the desks and chairs in two rows down opposite sides of the room.

3 Give each student a number: one, two, or three. Ask all the 1s to sit down the left-hand side of the room and all the twos to sit down the right-hand side opposite their partner. The threes can hover in the middle.

4 Explain that they are going to role play three situations, each involving an argument between two people, one and two. One and two will not speak to each other directly, but should make their views known to three who will help them to try and find a compromise solution.

5 Give out the cards for the first situation and ask the threes to go and listen to the ones.

6 When they have heard the ones' side of things, they should go and explain it to the twos, listen to their reply, and report back to the 1s, trying all the time to help the ones and twos reach a compromise agreement on settling their differences. This mediation should go on until both sides reach a satisfactory agreement.

7 Then get ones and threes to change places and continue with role play two.

8 Get the twos and threes to change places for role play three.

ROLE PLAY 1

> **Flatmate 1**
> Your flatmate is very inconsiderate: never does the washing-up and holds late-night parties in his room. He knows you have to get up early!

> **Flatmate 2**
> Your flatmate is very inconsiderate; he insists on keeping a dog which barks early in the morning. He knows you get up late!
> And he is much too tidy—always clearing your things away so that you can't find them.

ROLE PLAY 2

> **Neighbour 1**
> Your next-door neighbour always parks her car right in front of your driveway. It's very annoying, because it means that you can't get your car in and out of the drive.

> **Neighbour 2**
> Your neighbour's house is always full of visitors. It's very annoying, because they often make a lot of noise just when you want to do some work, but also because they park their cars all down the street and it's hard for you to find a parking place.

ROLE PLAY 3

> **Parent**
> You are having a row with your teenage daughter. You think she is too young to go to parties and come back late at night.

> **Daughter**
> You are having a row with your parents. They won't let you go out to friends' parties, and say you are too young to stay out late. It's not fair—all your friends go to parties!

17.4 Timetabling priorities

LEVEL

Lower-intermediate and above

TIME

20–30 minutes

MATERIALS

Set of role cards (see below) **and blank timetable for each group**

PROCEDURE

1 Give out the role cards, ensuring as far as possible that each student gets a role which is as far removed from their real language priorities as possible. For example, give a grammar buff a speaking role card. (You can find out about your students' priorities by doing the questionnaire in 2.2, 'What kind of language learner are you?')

2 Give one student in each group the 'observer' card, and ask them to note down what is said, and how the group arrives at a compromise.

3 Ask the groups to discuss how they would organize a timetable for their week's English course. Ask them to try a 'win–win' negotiation, concentrating on how they help each other achieve their aims rather than how they can achieve their own aims.

4 When they have reached an agreement, ask the observer to give them feedback on the processes they went through to achieve that agreement, and to discuss in their group how they felt about those processes.

5 Ask each group for comments on solutions and on the processes of compromise.

ROLE CARDS

> You are a student on a one-week course in England. You want to study grammar: it's important to speak a language correctly, otherwise people won't understand you when you speak.

> You are a student on a one-week course in England. You want to improve your speaking skills—you know the grammar but you can't speak fluently.

> You are a student on a one-week course in England. You want to improve your reading. You need to do a lot of reading for your job and you need to read much faster. You don't really need speaking or listening.

> You are a student on a one-week course in England. Your problem is vocabulary: you know quite enough about grammar, but you just haven't got enough words to discuss serious things properly.

> You are a student on a one-week course in England. Your main problem is your pronunciation. You'd like to concentrate on pronunciation practice and really improve!

> **Observer**
> Listen to the group discussion and take notes. Try to find out:
> – What each person wants.
> – What reasons they put forward for their opinions.
> – What suggestions are made to solve the conflict.
> – How people react to those suggestions.
> – How the problem is solved in the end.

17.5 Negotiating the timetable

LEVEL

Post-elementary and above

TIME

Half to one lesson

PROCEDURE

You can do this week by week, or establish an outline for the term, subject to periodic review. Simply ask the students, given their different priorities and needs, to say how the timetable should be organized and what weight should be given to different course components. Remind them of the ways they arrived at creative compromise solutions in the role play exercises and ask them to apply those techniques to their discussion. You can be involved in the discussion, or leave them to it, as you and they prefer. State your own opinions if you feel you have a right to a say in the matter too! They might like to take into consideration, for example, what you feel happiest doing, and what you think will help them most.

REMARKS

It is not fair, on the students or on you, to do this too early in the course, before they have had a chance to see what is on offer. To ask them what they want to do on the first day of the course is rather like asking someone what they want to drink, without telling them what you've got in the cupboard! Before you begin timetable negotiations, it is a good idea to do at least some of the following things:

- Teach a number of lessons involving different activities and focusing on different skills, so that the students have a good idea of what there is on offer and what they might find useful.
- Find out about student aims, preferences, and differences via some of the activities in Chapter 2, 'Thinking about language'.
- Begin to establish a friendly group atmosphere, with ice-breakers, gap-bridging, and trust activities.
- Get students to clarify their aims (see Chapter 16, 'A sense of direction').
- Prepare for the process of negotiation and compromise with one or two of the compromise activities in this chapter.

18 Coping with crisis: some group problems

Introduction

So far this book has been concerned with ways of trying to pre-empt potential problems with groups. In this chapter I want to take a brief look at what happens when such attempts fail. The first point I want to make is that you are not alone, and that your difficulties are not necessarily the result of inexperience or inadequacy on your part: the examples in this chapter were all given to me by experienced teachers, teacher trainers, and heads of department. The second point is that conflict and confrontation are not necessarily negative experiences, and may indeed lead to a very positive outcome. Finally, not all group problems are resolvable. While I do believe that most potential problems can be solved, or better, pre-empted by the use of techniques such as those in this book, the belief that the teacher is responsible for every group problem can lead to much unnecessary guilt and soul-searching. By offering a classification of some typical group problems, together with case studies of actual examples of those problems, and a tentative outline of strategies for coping with crisis, I hope to offer some help, or at least a feeling of solidarity, to the teacher experiencing difficulties with a group.

Sources of problems in groups

Answers to a second questionnaire, 'Moaning and Groaning 2', on problems experienced with groups, and strategies (successful and unsuccessful) for dealing with them, suggest that there are three main potential sources for problems with groups: teacher–group conflict, intra-group conflict, and the 'indigestible' group member (see diagram). The case studies below, taken from replies to the questionnaire, illustrate these.

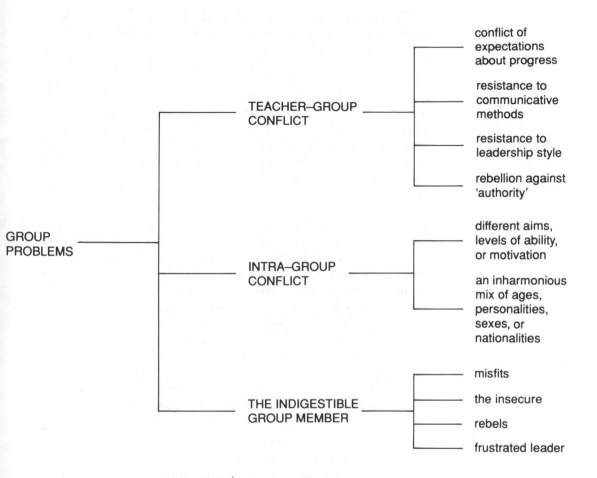

Teacher–group conflict

Case studies

1 A group of intermediate learners who had made good progress as beginners the term before. They were an above-average intermediate group and I was happy with their progress and thought they were too. About half-way through the term I became aware of subterranean discontent which surfaced in a complaint that they thought they weren't learning anything. I tried to reassure them that they were in fact doing very well, that they couldn't expect to learn as fast as when they were beginners, and gave them lots of counselling on 'intermediate learning plateaux', but without much success: they seemed to have suffered a fatal loss of confidence in themselves as learners and me as teacher. This, of course, *did* affect their learning and they began not to do so well. Very sad really as they were basically a good group who were learning well, but nothing I said seemed to convince them that you can't make the jump from being just post-beginner to talking in depth about politics and philosophy in a few weeks!

2 Eighteen- to twenty-year-old Turkish- and Arabic-speaking students used to authoritarian teachers who dictate content and expect regurgitation, and demand deference and respect. They had been assigned a new British female teacher (me) with a 'mission' to help the group enjoy learning and take responsibility for their own learning as befits university-level students. Before the crisis I had thought things were going well and a good atmosphere had been established. I had consulted them and asked their opinion, but didn't at that stage realize they were only answering as they thought I wanted; to please the teacher being their most important role. Then one day there was a burst of Turkish and a violent quarrel began. I asked them to argue in English at least, but to no avail. I left the room. Five minutes later the class asked me to return and explained that they *needed* me to be more authoritarian, to stop them talking, make them work, etc. After this crisis I revised my strategies and became more dictatorial because *they* had asked. There was more of a group feeling, though relations were always slightly strained.

3 A group of fourteen students, mostly aged 18–20, nearly all European, fairly advanced. They had been educated in the formal European tradition and reacted very negatively to 'communicative' methods. My solution was learner training (Ellis and Sinclair style), but this was only partly successful. In the end we compromised: I included more formal language work and also used a lot of intellectually stimulating materials—articles from journals, sessions on British culture, literature, etc. This worked well and they seemed happy.

4 Several composite mental pictures of group crises I've encountered include speaking loudly, shouting, interrupting, refusal to work, name-calling, walkout, student lying on teacher's desk and singing, group throwing chairs and prising tiles off the floor (these last from a group I had years ago in FE college— Hmm! I'd almost forgotten about them!). Unsuccessful dealings on my part include me fleeing and returning with head of department, threatening, talking a lot, explaining, defending, apologizing, pleading—they never work!

Comments

Teacher–group conflicts are in many ways the most painful group experience for teachers, who can feel attacked, exposed, and hurt that their ideas, teaching style, and methodology have been rejected. Problems of ideology, humiliation, and hurt pride can complicate the situation and get in the way of finding a suitable solution. These situations can end in bitterness and frustration for all concerned. The case studies above demonstrate some of the most common sources of teacher–group conflicts: unrealistic expectations about progress (1); resistance to the teacher's leadership style and student role (2) (students can also, of course, resist a style they see as too authoritarian, and demand more democracy but interestingly in EFL, the reverse often seems to be the case); resistance to communicative methods (3), and rebellion for its own sake (as distinct from demanding more classroom democracy) (4). In case studies 2 and 3 the problem was alleviated by the teacher listening carefully, taking account of cultural differences which led to a mismatch of teacher and student expectations, and compromising by changing her own leadership style and teaching methods, or adapting them to form a hybrid between learner expectations and the teacher's preferred style. Careful listening and flexibility on the part of the teacher are vital—even if it means swallowing your pride and your principles. In case study 1 the teacher possibly fell into the trap of explaining and justifying too much: the students were convinced they had a real problem, so it became a real problem; the teacher denying that there was a problem resulted in a deadlock. Case study 4 also warns against too much explaining and defending.

Intra-group conflict

Case studies

5 A group of mixed nationalities. The higher end of the group were taking FCE at the end of term. A couple of the group badly needed basic language work, and others needed oral practice, while the younger students wanted to read newspapers, discuss politics, etc. By mid-term the needs of the group had diverged to such an extent that many of the group were feeling very discontented. We sat down and discussed it and I held individual tutorials where I suggested extra activities the higher level students could do to help themselves. In the end we reached a consensus on certain class activities which we all regarded as useful and I increased the amount of self-access work they did. This helped to alleviate the problem, but didn't solve it, since it was insoluble.

6 A group consisting of half majority nationality and half ethnic minority from the same country. Half-way through term I became uncomfortably aware of two factions developing. I realized this was partly my fault through not keeping seating fluid or mixing groups enough. I tried some group-building activities, tensions eased and things got better, but I was still not completely happy with the situation. Then someone in the school organized an inter-class football match, and the problem vanished: inter-group rivalry—perhaps the most powerful group-maintaining feeling!

7 Three groups of young Japanese students divided according to ability and consisting of a mixture of well-motivated, hard-working students and a bunch of real rebels who were constantly

making trouble, and disrupting learning for the others. Talking and reasoning with them did not work and they confounded all our attempts at creating some sort of group identity. Teaching spoken English was a real struggle and I tended to get them to read and write as it was less of a battle. At the end of the first term a radical decision was taken, to regroup the classes on the basis of motivation rather than ability, so that students who were well motivated would not be held back by those who were fooling around. Term 2 was in some ways easier, the 'top' group was a much more pleasant place to spend 40 minutes, but the 'bottom' group was uncontrollable. I felt so demoralized by the whole experience that I resigned at the end of term.

Comments

Problem 5 is of a different nature from problems 6 and 7. Problem 5 is a rational problem and can be solved, as it was, by rational means: discussion, negotiation, and compromise. Problems 6 and 7 are irrational, stemming from emotions such as dislike, fear, and irritation in group members. Confronting the problem head on and talking it through will work with a basically well-balanced group or with a minor upset, but with a deep-rooted problem or very extreme behaviour it is not likely to do much good, unless you are a trained psychotherapist, and you may find yourself getting into emotional deep water. Similarly, affective activities of the gap-bridging, group identity type will work only if the disharmony in the group is below a certain critical level, as in problem 6. However, once that level is reached, these activities can be counterproductive or even explosive, as the teacher in problem 7 found. This teacher found that the only way to cope with her groups was in fact to do the very reverse of group-forming activities: to 'lower the temperature' by including a higher proportion of traditional controlled exercises and individualizing work. Sometimes a radical decision to regroup students on a different basis may be the only way to create a less explosive mixture of people. Obviously, all these measures were felt by the teachers to be unsatisfactory. The solution that intrigues me most is the one of the football match, or a kind of *deus ex machina* solution. I have a feeling that this kind of sideways, unexpected, apparently irrelevant solution may be the best answer to a log-jam, where head-on confrontation of a problem is yielding no results. The trouble with *dei* is that they are not always available when you need them! It is always worth thinking laterally and considering the unexpected or unlikely response when faced with an unresolvable deadlock. At the very least, it probably won't make matters any worse.

The 'indigestible' group member

Case studies

8 A success story but this is not really *my* strategy, it was the group's strategy: a lively, affectionate, happy class of beginners with one very shy and awkward student with a stammer and obvious learning problems. I was just beginning to realize that he had fairly serious learning disabilities and was partially dyslexic and wondering how to cope, when I became aware that the class had quietly, unobtrusively, taken charge of the problem themselves. By some unspoken but generally agreed arrangement, they would take it in turns to sit with him during the lessons. His partner for that lesson would virtually renounce his own learning in order to explain and go over things with him. He was treated with very great affection by everyone in the class, like a favourite younger child in a family, and when they discovered his talent for drawing he was constantly in demand to produce cartoons of teachers and other students. Under this warm and gentle atmosphere he really blossomed, and though he never made great progress with English his increase in confidence was remarkable.

9 An older refugee, obviously traumatized by his experiences, in a group of young Europeans, who at first tended to ignore him and focus on their own interests. They didn't ostracize him, they were just unthinking. I became concerned about his isolation, and did two things: I voiced my concern to the rest of the group and organized a session which allowed him to talk about what was on his mind—the situation in his country and what it was like to live there. The younger students had not really been aware of his isolation, and when it was pointed out to them, and especially when they heard about the troubles in his country, did their best to involve him. This led to a slightly artificial situation at first, a bit like a polite vicarage tea-party, but through it he became much more a part of the group and developed a real and lasting friendship with a young couple.

10 A teacher who arrived late on an overseas teachers' refresher course. She had been on a course in Britain once before and talked of nothing else, objecting to everything that was done with, 'This isn't what we did in X', or 'Oh, but in X we . . .'. Annoying as this was, we realized that she probably felt anxious and insecure through arriving late in an already formed group and this was a way of impressing her identity on the group. We gave a lot of time and energy to giving her the attention she wanted and to integrating her securely in the group, and also, when she was secure enough, teased her (affectionately) about her constant nostalgia for X. Once she had found her place in the group, she became an enthusiastic participant and we didn't hear any more about X.

11 The indigestible group member—yes! Dominates talk, shows off knowledge, dresses very provocatively, turns up volume, seeks attention, holds principles that are absolutely counter to those of the group-leader and so gets very very angry at the way things are done.

12 An intermediate group, mixed nationalities, predominantly young, male, and European. X was older, an extrovert and self-confident Japanese man who had been at the school longer than most of the others. He was attention-seeking, domineering, and argumentative in class. The other students, being younger, were impressed by his self-confidence but irritated by his domineering manner. One girl moved classes because he was so rude to her. As the term progressed his influence increased. He organized a 'study group' at his house to work for the exam and at the same time fomented a lot of discontent about what was going on in class and a lot of panic about the exam. About four weeks before the end of term (and the exam) he suddenly withdrew from the course (on financial grounds, he said). The group immediately became happier, and more harmonious and responsive.

13 The one who still stands out in my mind as the classic indigestible student, I shall call T. He was the bane of my life for six months or more. He was very disruptive and sometimes actually violent: he and a friend beat up one of the quieter members of the class. Basically, we found that confronting T did not work—we were all in the end quite wary of his violent behaviour. The only strategy for coping with him was to ignore him—none of us felt happy about this but in the end we gave up the struggle to understand and help him because he gave nothing in return. At the end of term we refused to take him back for another term.

14 A real rebel, with a quieter 'accomplice' who allowed himself to be led on, constantly disrupted lessons, arrived late, refused to talk English, chatted instead of working, etc. They didn't get the reaction they wanted (admiration? attention?) from the group who instead made a point of deliberately ostracizing them, saying things like, 'I'm not going to work with them, they don't do any work'. Within a short time they settled down and became much pleasanter people to work with. Peer group pressure is much more powerful than teacher pressure!

Comments

The above examples demonstrate different ways in which people can be indigestible: problems 8 and 9 concern social misfits, people who deviate strongly from the norm of the group. If you have a fairly normal group, it should be possible to integrate these people, unless there is something seriously wrong. In some cases the group will do it for you in its own way, in other cases, they may need a gentle reminder. Integrating a misfit can actually improve the cohesion of a group by giving them a shared social responsibility.

Problem 10 is an example of someone who is attention-seeking and disruptive, merely because she is insecure. If such a person is given warmth and the attention they are seeking and helped to integrate into the group, they will usually stop being a nuisance fairly soon.

Frustrated leaders, on the other hand, can be extremely difficult for the teacher to deal with, particularly if they succeed in influencing a weak group. Alternatively, a strong group may unite to reject the frustrated leader as in 14. It is important to distinguish this problem from genuine teacher–group problems which can be solved by discussion—the frustrated leader may find you in the wrong whatever you do. The best way to find out which situation you are dealing with is by giving individual interviews at an early stage, and by insisting in any group discussion that everyone gives their own opinion and says 'I think . . .' instead of 'We all think . . .'.

Problems 13 and 14 are obvious examples of rebels. If you have or can create a strong group, they will deal with the problem as in 14. Getting to know the rebel, and making sure she or he knows you, can help: it is difficult to treat someone as an abstract symbol of authority if you actually know them personally. Sometimes confrontation can provide the limits the rebel is seeking, or shock him or her into reassessing the situation, though it could also harden attitudes and make the problem worse. But the teachers in the case of 13 found themselves in a situation where neither reasoning nor confrontation worked and the problem was too extreme to be dealt with by the group. In this case, as in 7, the problem seemed incapable of harmonious resolution and ended only with the extreme solution of disbanding the group or expulsion of one disruptive student. In each case the teachers seemed to blame themselves, admitting to feelings of guilt, inadequacy, unhappiness, or complete demoralization.

In the following pages I will try to suggest different levels of response to group problems, and some strategies for defusing tension in conflicts and achieving a compromise solution.

Responding to problems

Some problems are relatively easy to solve, requiring a minimum of discussion. Others are more deep-rooted and may lead to a difficult confrontation. Sometimes you may judge it better to avoid confrontation altogether. The following four levels of response to group problems offer an opportunity of solving them at each level.

Level 1

At an early stage in the group life, i.e. when there is still a potential rather than an actual problem, try to pre-empt the problem by using both cognitive and affective exercises as suggested in this book. Different groups will obviously require different emphases and activities; a group made up of very different personalities may benefit from gap-bridging and group-identity activities, for example, while a group with differing aims may benefit from the more cognitive goal-defining and compromise activities.

Level 2

At the same time open up a channel for keeping in touch with the opinions, feelings, and reactions of individual students. One way of doing this is to take one lesson for individual interviews of five to ten minutes each: set the class a writing or self-access task (a language lab session is ideal) and ask students to come for individual interviews in turn, preferably in a place where they cannot be overheard by others. Ask for feedback on feelings about the course, teaching techniques, their progress so far, the group atmosphere. This is a good way of sorting out individual problems which cannot be dealt with in the group, and if you have students from very different cultures it will give them the chance to tell you of particular difficulties they are experiencing. If the interviews suggest that there is a problem brewing, go to Level 3; if not, as in the vast majority of classes, return happily to Level 1.

Level 3

At this point you have four courses available to you.

1 'Soldiering on' involves doing exactly what you were doing before in the hope that the problem will go away or resolve itself. If the problem is minor or temporary in nature (for example, a minor tiff between two group members, or an unfavourable reaction to one lesson) this is what will probably happen. In the case of a more deep-rooted problem such as a feud between group members or group dissatisfaction with the course, this is probably the worst thing you could do.

2 'Avoiding friction' entails a change in teaching style or emphasis, so that there is less contact between group members and a lower emotional temperature.

3 'Breaking the mould' involves more radical solutions such as regrouping students, changing teachers or tactics, and the possibility of a 'lateral' solution which focuses group energy more productively in a different direction. In the case of a deeply rooted emotional problem or extreme irrational or violent behaviour, you may decide that you do not want confrontation. It is important to draw the line between teaching and psychotherapy! You may also be teaching students from a culture where open confrontation is always avoided, who might find our society's stress on 'clearing the air' and 'bringing things out into the open' very disturbing. In these cases, 'Avoiding friction' or 'Breaking the mould' may be your best options.

4 'Confronting the problem' is in many ways the hardest solution. It carries the highest risk, but also a good chance of providing a real solution, provided that you are able successfully to defuse tension and focus the group's energy on solutions rather than grievances. In the case of an 'ideas' conflict (for instance, difference of opinion on teaching methods or course design) it should be your first choice; an emotional or personality difference may be harder to deal with in this way, though it is often better to get things out in the open than to leave them to fester. Pride, selfishness, or rigid ideology complicate problems and cloud the issues, and even if you think you are confronting a conflict of opinions, you will probably find yourself dealing with emotions as well. The choice of whether to confront the problem or not may not be left to you in any case—the group may decide to bring matters to a head itself. See the next section on 'Strategies for coping with conflict' for a more detailed discussion of ways of confronting the problem.

Level 4

If the crisis has been resolved, you and the group should be able to enter a new phase of productive work. Depending on the solution this may mean keeping the same methods and style, or it may mean a modification of your teaching style, methods used, or way the timetable is divided up. If the solution is a true consensus solution you should have a new atmosphere in the group and a willingness to work.

It may happen, though, that your best attempts to resolve the crisis fail and the group cannot be reconciled. In this case you will have to return to Level 3 and try one of the other solutions there. Like the teachers quoted in the previous section, you may feel guilty, inadequate, or demoralized: somehow as teachers we have the feeling that we *ought* to be able to resolve all human conflict, and if we meet a problem that defies out best efforts to solve it we have failed in our job. Whatever gave us this idea? In this context I would like to quote a reply to the questionnaire (from a senior teacher trainer):

> Your questionnaire arrived at a time when I was experiencing the most difficult class I have taught in 25 years in the classroom. With all my training and experience, I was forced in the end to say, 'I don't understand anything that is going on here', and letting go of the need to understand and work things out was the only honest thing for me to do. It did not make the loneliness and inadequacy go away, but it did make me see my limitations and enable me to get in touch with my humility ... this group at least helped me to realize that it is a kind of arrogance for me to think that I am able to handle *every* classroom situation that comes my way—or even understand it. So the most 'difficult' group may well have turned out the most valuable for my learning and personal development.

Some strategies for coping with conflict

This section proposes some possible strategies and techniques for defusing tension, exploring points of view, and arriving at a workable solution to a conflict. Some may be more useful with certain groups and situations. Some groups may be adept at managing their own confrontations. It is up to you to select and use those that you and your group feel comfortable with. Your attitude to confrontation will be crucial. If you view it as a chance to make positive changes rather than as a negative and difficult experience, then the confrontation is more likely to be constructive and yield positive results.

Listening

One source of tension in conflicts is that people are so intent on putting forward their own point of view that they do not listen properly to others. Here are some guidelines for good listening:

- Really make an effort to listen to what the speaker is saying instead of mentally preparing your own counter-arguments while he or she is talking.
- Make eye contact with the person who is speaking.
- Show that you are listening by body language; don't betray irritation or impatience.
- Don't interrupt and don't react defensively as soon as the speaker stops.
- Instead of leaping in immediately with your own counter-arguments, acknowledge what the speaker has said in some way, make a positive comment if you can, or ask for an explanation of anything you didn't quite understand.

If the conflict is between you and the group, you should adopt these strategies yourself; if it is an intra-group conflict, you will have to make these 'rules' explicit to the group.

Stating your case

Conflicts can become inflamed by personal accusations, wild generalizations, and overstatement. You can help to reduce inflammatory remarks by following these guidelines:

- Insist that participants in the debate say 'I think', 'I feel', not 'We all . . .'.
- Discourage people from making direct and hurtful accusations. A good way of doing this is by insisting that instead of making statements beginning 'You' and focusing on the other person's behaviour, people make statements beginning 'I' and focusing on their own reactions to that behaviour. For instance, instead of saying 'You're very selfish, always coming late and talking in French', say, 'I get distracted when you talk in French and then I can't think in English any more'.
- Don't allow generalizations, ask people to be very specific. Instead of accepting, 'You don't teach us properly', get them to say something like, 'I (not we!) don't enjoy pairwork because I feel it's very artificial'.
- If things get overheated or the argument starts to go round in unproductive circles, take a break by asking the group to write instead of speak or playing some music and asking them to close their eyes and relax for a few minutes.

Making sure all views are represented

Discussions can easily get taken over by a vociferous and opinionated minority and it can be hard to get more timid or less passionate group members to put forward their opinions. Make sure everyone has a chance to speak and that no one is allowed to speak 'on behalf of' others. If more reticent members are getting drowned out or seem reluctant to contribute publicly, structure the discussion differently, for instance as a pyramid discussion (see 12.1), or ask them to write and then give a summary of what they have written (see Chapter 14, 'Ensuring participation'). You can also hold individual interviews.

Seeing the other point of view

This, of course, is the stumbling block in most conflicts! Ask people to summarize what has just been said before they reply to it: this may seem a bit laborious or artificial, but it ensures they really listen, helps prevent misinterpretation, and slows down hasty defensive reactions. Try empathy techniques: get Faction A to present Faction B's views as if they were Faction B, and Faction B to reply as if they were Faction A (see Chapter 7).

Finding a solution

This, of course, is the aim of the whole process, but it is important to get all opinions thoroughly aired first, otherwise resentment will remain and be detrimental to the search for a solution. It is important to establish that everyone has said all they want to about the problem before beginning to work on a solution, though obviously the debate must be stopped if it begins to go round in circles and repeat itself. To find out if everyone has had their say on the issue, summarize the various positions (notes on the board will help) and ask if anyone has anything *new* to add. The process of finding a solution should be a win–win negotiation, not a win–lose negotiation: it is important to reach a consensus solution, not a majority vote. A majority–minority decision will leave some members feeling permanently discontented and may make the split in your group even more apparent than it was before. It is important to establish the idea that you are looking for a win–win solution before you begin negotiations. Before you begin the actual process of negotiating a compromise, try one of the following:

Solution visualization
Play some gentle music as a background, and ask students to close their eyes and try to visualize a positive outcome to the dispute, a solution that would make them feel happy and make the class an enjoyable place to be. Ask them to open their eyes and to tell the person sitting next to them about the outcome they visualized. Then ask each pair to tell the group about their vision for the future. This exercise redirects energy from negative feelings to positive ones in order to prepare the ground for a more constructive discussion.

Brainstorming solutions
Divide the group into pairs and give each pair a pile of small pieces of paper. Ask them to think of as many possible solutions to the problem as possible and to write them down on the pieces of paper: one idea per piece of paper. Set a time-limit. They should write down whatever comes into their head, however unlikely or bizarre the suggestion seems. They should not reject ideas simply because they don't agree with them, but write everything down. When the time-limit is up, stop them and ask everyone to contribute suggestions. Write them all on the board.

This exercise is a way of getting group members to think laterally and see possibilities outside their own point of view.

Either of these exercises could lead straight into the process of negotiating a consensus solution. If you have done some of the exercises from Chapter 17 with your group already, the students will be familiar with the idea of win–win negotiations; if not you will have to explain. This negotiation can be done as a whole-group discussion, or if you prefer, as a pyramid discussion (see 12.1) or in the following format:

Divide the class into three small groups, A, B, and C. Ask them to discuss their preferred solutions to the problem, using the ideas from the brainstorm or visualization as a starting point, and to try to come up with a solution they all feel happy with. Then ask one person from group A to go to B, one person from B to go to C, and one person from C to go to A, and to compare solutions. (Choose conciliatory rather than aggressive people for this role.) Ask them to try and find a compromise between the two solutions, and then to return to their group and discuss it. Their group, meanwhile, will have negotiated a different compromise with another group, so a compromise will have to be found between the two compromises! Finally, ask one member of A to go to C, one member of B to go to A, and one member of C to go to B to compare their compromise solutions. This should be easier since each group should have negotiated roughly the same sort of compromise. Ask them to report back to their groups and make any further modifications they want to their solutions. Then open out the discussion to involve the whole group and finalize the solution.

This way of structuring the discussion means that compromises are arrived at in stages: the small steps involved may be easier to negotiate than the large task of finding a group consensus through public discussion.

Afterword

This has been a chapter which largely focused on negative experience, so I would like to end with a more positive one, an anecdote told to me by another teacher: a reminder that your perception of the success or failure of your efforts may not in the end be the right one:

> One overseas teachers' course on Communicative Language Teaching was made extremely difficult for me by one of the participants whom I shall call Gerhard Fischbein. Gerhard did not take to Communicative Language Teaching. He objected, loudly and rudely, to almost everything I did on the course. He had a deep distrust of communicative methodology, challenged the principles, refused to take part in the exercises, and ruined the atmosphere for everyone.

About a year later I was in Germany to hold a seminar for
secondary school teachers. In the lobby of the institution
where I was to give the workshop I passed a noticeboard
advertising a forthcoming course. In large red letters it said
'Communicative Language Teaching: Principles and Practice.
Course tutor: Gerhard Fischbein'.

Acknowledgements
Many of the strategies decribed in this section derive from
counselling techniques. *The Red Book of Groups* (Houston 1984)
is a useful and stimulating source of further techniques.

Section C
Ending the group experience

Introduction

If a group has been close and affectionate, it is easy for them to feel let down, abandoned, and lost at the end of a course, when the group life is over and everyone disperses. It is important to give students some sense of continuity after the abrupt end of a course that may have been a major part of their lives for some three months, or even longer. Two areas are important here: keeping up the English they have learned, and keeping up the friendships they have made.

A 'group brainstorm' on ways of learning English after the course is over is a useful way of pooling ideas: students will be able to suggest ideas that may not have occurred to others in the group. Also, they may not know of sources of authentic English that you can suggest to them, for example the BBC World Service, *Authentik in English* magazine, or the English language magazines *Click, Clockwork, Current*, and *Catch* published by Mary Glasgow. (See 'Further reading' section for addresses.)

Keeping up friendship networks is also important: students will probably organize a class or school address list, but may also like the idea of 'Round robins', where one student writes a paragraph about what he or she has been doing, and sends it to another student, who adds a paragraph about him or herself and sends it on to a third student, and so on. The list for this will need to be organized in advance and the end of term is an ideal time for doing so.

The activities in this section are designed to round off the group experience in a way that is positive and forward-looking, so that the students not only remember the high points of the course, and have a chance to express their thanks to and feelings for other group members, but can also evaluate what they've learned, identify areas for further work, and look forward both to continuing learning English and to keeping in contact with the friends they have made on the course.

19 Ending with positive feelings

It is nice to end the term on a positive note, and give students a chance to express their feelings towards one another. The activities in this section allow the students to look back over the group experience and indulge in a little nostalgic reminiscing.

19.1 Remember when...?

LEVEL

All

TIME

20 minutes

MATERIALS

Pile of small slips of paper for each student

PROCEDURE

1 Give each student a pile of small slips of paper.

2 Write on the board 'Remember when...?' and ask the students to think back over nice or funny things that have happened to the group in the course of the term.

3 Ask them to complete the sentence in as many ways as possible, one sentence-ending per slip of paper.

4 After they have been writing a little time, ask them to join up with a partner and share their sentences, and go on writing, jogging each others' memories.

5 Then ask everyone in the class to share their memories.

6 It is a good idea, if you have time so near the end of term, to collect in the sentences, type them up, and make a copy for each student as a souvenir.

VARIATION

1 Ask students to relax and close their eyes. Play gentle music if you like. Ask the students to let pictures come into their minds of incidents they have enjoyed during the term. Ask them to try to get a vivid mental picture of the first incident or scene involving themselves or other people in the group and then to imagine a succession of such pictures, like a private snapshot album. Ask them to imagine turning the pages and seeing the pictures.

2 Give them time to imagine each picture and then ask them to open their eyes and turn to the person sitting next to them and to share the contents of their mental photo album.

19.2 I'll remember them because...

LEVEL All

TIME 20 minutes

PREPARATION Prepare a short description of everyone in the class, as in the example below.

PROCEDURE 1 Start by giving the class a mystery description of someone in the class, for example: 'She's a small slim girl in her mid-twenties, always fashionably dressed. I'll remember her because she was as shy as a mouse when she first arrived and she's really noisy now!'

2 Ask the students to write a complimentary description of two or three people in the class, without mentioning their names. Like yours, their description should end 'I'll remember her (him) because...'.

3 When they have finished, ask them to read their descriptions out, and let the others guess who it is. Inevitably, some students will get a higher profile than others: intersperse the students' texts with your own, to ensure that everyone in the class gets mentioned at least once.

4 Again, if you have the time and energy to type some of these up and copy them, they make a nice souvenir.

19.3 Thank-you presents

LEVEL All

TIME 20 minutes

PROCEDURE 1 Ask students to think about the other people in the group and to make a list of their names.

2 Ask them to think of something they would particularly like to thank each person for, and to imagine an appropriate present that they would like to give them. Give an example: 'I would like to thank Johann for making us laugh so much together, and I would like to give him a bumper book of jokes and a clown's hat, and I would like to thank Almudena for wearing such colourful clothes on rainy days, and I would like to give her a shocking pink micro skirt.'

3 When they have finished their lists, ask them to read them out.

19.4 Hopes for the future

LEVEL

All

TIME

20 minutes

PROCEDURE

1 Ask each student in the class to think about the other students and to imagine them all in five years' time.

2 Ask them to write down their hopes for everyone in the class, for example: 'I hope Fatima will have realized her dream of becoming a journalist'; 'I hope Juan-Carlos will marry Silvia and that they will have a lovely baby.'

3 When they have finished, ask everyone to read out their hopes.

VARIATION

1 Ask students to close their eyes. Ask them to imagine that in twenty years' time, the class have decided to have a reunion.

2 Ask them the following questions, giving them time to visualize the answers:

– Where is the reunion—in which town or country?
– What do you all decide to do together: a meal? a dance? a walk in the country?
– What has happened to everyone in the meantime?

3 Say everyone's name in turn and ask students to imagine they are talking to that person and finding out what they have been doing during the last twenty years.

4 Then ask students to open their eyes and tell the person sitting next to them about their reunion. Open the discussion out to involve the whole group by asking everyone to tell the group one interesting, funny, or surprising thing about 'their' reunion.

20 Evaluating the group experience

As well as allowing students the opportunity to express their feelings for each other and to indulge in a little nostalgia, you may like to encourage them to take a more clear-sighted look at what they have done during the term and to begin to formulate their goals for future language learning. (With some groups, however, the last week of term is not a good time to ask for rational analysis and evaluation—witness the responses to the 'Old Lags' Project'!)

20.1 Look how far we've come

LEVEL

All (though this works best with elementary and intermediate groups, where progress is most dramatic)

TIME

20 minutes

MATERIALS

Tape-recording of students at beginning of course, or uncorrected work from early on in the course

PROCEDURE

Play a tape-recording of students speaking in the early days of the course, or give them back some uncorrected work from the first week or so of the course. Students are usually pleasantly surprised at the progress they have made. This is a good morale booster at the end of a course.

20.2 Now we can...

LEVEL

All

TIME

20 minutes

PROCEDURE

1 Bring the students' original list of aims for the term (see 16.3, 'What do I want?') and ask them to tick off those they feel they have gone at least some way towards achieving.

2 Ask them to discuss their aims with a partner.

3 Then open up the discussion to the whole class.

REMARKS

This activity leads well into the next one.

20.3 Evaluating learning strategies

LEVEL   **Elementary and above**

TIME   **15–20 minutes**

MATERIALS   **One copy of the questionnaire for each student**

PROCEDURE   **1** Give a copy of the questionnaire to each student and ask them to fill it in.

2 When they have finished, ask them to share their ideas with a partner and finally to summarize their ideas to the group as a whole.

QUESTIONNAIRE

WHAT LEARNING STRATEGIES WERE MOST USEFUL TO ME?

Number the following activities according to how much they helped you to learn English. (1=most useful for me, 11=least useful for me)

learning vocabulary lists by heart ☐

doing grammar exercises ☐

translating ☐

listening to people talking ☐

listening to tapes and answering questions ☐

listening to the radio or TV ☐

practising reading skills ☐

writing compositions or letters ☐

speaking to people ☐

language lab ☐

reading books or stories for pleasure ☐

Which activities will be possible for you to continue using after the course is over, if you have to study on your own? Put a circle round these.

Now compare your answers with a friend and discuss which strategies will be most useful to you when the course is over.

20.4 What's left to do?

LEVEL	**All**
TIME	**20 minutes**
PROCEDURE	Ask students individually to try to identify areas they still need to work on and to try to clarify their future language learning goals. What goals from their original list do they feel they have not yet achieved? What weaknesses do they feel they still have? What are their new goals?

20.5 The old lags' letter

LEVEL	**Elementary and above**
TIME	**30–40 minutes**
PROCEDURE	Ask students to imagine they are writing a letter to a new student who will be beginning the course next term. Ask students to write and tell him or her what to expect, saying what they found surprising, what they enjoyed, what they found difficult, what they found worked for them, and giving them advice for learning English.
REMARKS	Some of these letters may prove a useful real introduction for incoming students in the new term.

21 Finale

At the end of a term, easy or difficult, with a group, it can also be a valuable experience for you to think back over the term and evaluate the progress of the group during the term and the strategies and techniques you used to promote good group dynamics. As a tailpiece to the book, here is a short self-evaluation questionnaire to help you think back over what happened during the term and analyse what worked and why.

SELF-EVALUATION QUESTIONNAIRE

1 Think about the composition of your group: how did this affect (a) the dynamics of the group, and (b) your leadership style?

2 Were you sufficiently aware of the nature of the group and willing to adjust your teaching style to suit them?

3 Think about the development of the group as the term progressed: can you divide this into stages?

4 Were you aware of these stages during the course: did you have to modify what you did to take account of them? How did you do this and was it successful?

5 Did group relations progress harmoniously and steadily or were there setbacks and crises?

6 What strategies did you use, consciously or unconsciously, to promote good group dynamics?

7 How and why did you select these strategies?

8 Were these successful or unsuccessful? Why?

9 In retrospect, do you think there was anything more you could have done, or a different strategy you could have tried, to improve group atmosphere?

10 How did you keep in touch with the feelings and opinions of (a) the class as a whole, (b) individuals in the class?
Is there any better way you could have done this?

11 How did you deal with any crises or problems that arose? Was the group atmosphere better or worse after this?

12 Try to analyse the causes of any problems. In retrospect, do you think there was anything more you could have done (a) to prevent the crisis happening, or (b) to defuse tension and find a solution?

13 Try, finally, to focus on something positive that you have gained or learned from the experience, something that will help you for the next group you encounter—who will, of course, be a completely different, unpredictable, complex, fascinating, and challenging group of individuals.

No people are uninteresting
Their fate is as the chronicle of planets

Nothing in them is not particular
And planet is dissimilar from planet

Yevtushenko

Language focus index

Index of topics

Abilities   1.5, 5.1, 5.2, 10.2

Comparing and contrasting   5.2, 8.5

Compliments   10.5

Countries and nationalities   4.1, 11.4

Describing actions   6.1, 9.1, 13.5

Describing people   1.1, 1.2, 1.3, 1.6, 1.7, 2.1, 4.2, 4.3, 5.1, 5.2, 6.4, 10.3, 11.5, 13.5

Describing places   1.4, 4.1, 11.4, 11.5, 13.2

Describing scenes   5.5, 13.5

Directions   5.1

Emotions   4.5, 7.4, 7.5, 9.1, 9.2, 9.3, 10.7

Families   1.6, 4.5, 8.6

General truths   4.2, 13.3

Habits and routines   4.3, 4.5, 6.2, 7.1, 7.5, 8.2, 10.1, 11.5

Hobbies   5.1, 8.2

Hopes   19.4

Hypothesis   7.2

Introductions   1.2, 5.3, 5.4

Invitations   5.6

Jobs   1.5, 5.3

Likes and dislikes   5.1, 8.2

Opinions   4.2, 5.1, 13.1

Opposites   2.1

Past events   6.3, 6.4, 6.5, 7.4, 8.2, 8.3, 8.4, 11.1, 11.3, 11.5, 19.1

Personal characteristics   1.3, 2.1, 4.3, 4.4, 4.5, 4.6, 4.7, 7.3, 8.2, 8.5, 10.2, 10.3, 10.4, 10.5, 19.1, 19.2

Personal history   7.3, 8.1, 8.2

Plans and intentions   6.7, 8.2, 16.1, 16.2, 19.4

Predictions   6.6, 11.2

Promises   9.4

Reasons   10.4, 10.6, 16.1, 19.2

Thanking   10.4, 19.3

Index of structures

Adjectives:
  positive   10.5
  describing emotions   7.4, 7.5, 9.2, 9.3, 10.7, 15.1, 15.2
  describing people   1.1, 1.7, 4.2, 4.3, 4.4, 5.1, 5.2, 7.3, 8.6, 10.3, 10.5, 11.5, 19.2
  describing places   1.4, 4.1, 5.5, 11.4, 11.5, 13.2, 17.1

To be   4.1, 5.1, 5.2, 5.5, 7.4, 9.2, 9.3, 10.7, 11.4, 11.5, 13.2

Because   7.1, 10.4, 10.6, 16.1, 19.2

Can   1.5, 5.1, 5.2, 10.2, 20.2

Comparatives and superlatives   5.2, 8.5, 13.3

Conditionals   1.5, 7.2, 9.4

Future:
  simple   6.6, 9.4, 11.2, 19.4
  continuous   6.6
  perfect   6.6, 19.4

Going to   5.6, 6.7

Have got   4.1, 5.1, 5.2, 5.5, 11.4, 13.2

Passives   13.3

Past:
  continuous   6.5, 11.3
  present perfect   6.3, 6.4, 11.3
  simple   6.3, 7.3, 7.4, 8.1, 8.2, 8.3, 8.4, 9.1, 9.2, 9.3, 11.1, 11.3, 11.5, 13.3, 15.1, 15.2, 17.2, 19.1
  Used to   4.6

Prepositions:
  place   5.1, 5.5, 13.2, 17.1

Note

The activities in 'Learning to listen' (15), 'A sense of direction' (16), and 'Coexistence and compromise' (17), as well as those in Chapters 1, 2, 3, and 20, are not primarily language practice activities and therefore have no particular language focus.

The activities in 'Bringing it together' (12) and 'Ensuring participation' (14) are designed to be used with discussions on a variety of possible topics.

Further reading

Background reading

The following books are mainly academic studies giving insights into the sociology and psychology of groups. The majority of the books are concerned with the functioning of groups in general (for example, family, work, friends, etc.), although McLeish, Schmuck, and Wright deal specifically with groups in the classroom. Gaie Houston's book is a little different, exploring the various techniques that lead to more effective group management.

Argyle, M. 1969. *Social Interaction*. London: Tavistock Press.
Argyle, M. 1972. *The Social Psychology of Work*. London: Penguin.
Belbin, R. M. 1981. *Management Teams*. Oxford: Heinemann.
Douglas, T. 1983. *Groups: Understanding People Together*. London: Tavistock Press.
Goffman, E. 1969. *The Presentation of Self in Everyday Life*. London: Penguin.
Hare, P. A. 1982. *Creativity in Small Groups*. London: Sage Publications.
Houston, G. 1990. *The Red Book of Groups*. London: G. Houston.
McLeish, J. 1973. *The Psychology of the Learning Group*. London: Hutchinson.
Schmuck, P. A. and **R. A. Schmuck.** 1976. *Group Processes in the Classroom*. Dubuque, IA: William Brown.
Sprott, W. J. H. 1958. *Human Groups*. London: Penguin.
Wright, T. 1987. *Roles of Teachers and Learners*. Oxford: Oxford University Press.

Ice-breakers and warm-ups

The Recipe Book has a useful section on 'warm-ups, breaks, and fillers'. The books listed in the 'Drama and trust activities' section are also good sources of ice-breakers.

Lindstromberg, S. 1990. *The Recipe Book*. London: Longman.

Humanistic techniques

The following books are useful and stimulating sources of exercises similar to those in Chapters 4, 6, 7, and 10. *Grammar Games* and *Grammar in Action* contain many 'personalized grammar' exercises, while the others can be used to develop speaking skills and simultaneously encourage the students to find out more about each other.

Baudins, M. and **R. Baudins**. 1990. *Alternatives*. London: Longman.
Deller, S. 1990. *Lessons from the Learner*. London: Longman.
Frank, C. and **M. Rinvolucri**. 1987. *Grammar in Action*. New York: Prentice Hall.
Klippel, F. 1985. *Keep Talking*. Cambridge: Cambridge University Press.
Morgan, J. and **M. Rinvolucri**. 1988. *The Q Book*. London: Longman.
Moskowitz, G. 1978. *Caring and Sharing in the Foreign Language Classroom*. Rowley, Mass.: Newbury House.
Porter-Ladousse, G. 1983. *Speaking Personally*. Cambridge: Cambridge University Press.
Rinvolucri, M. 1984. *Grammar Games*. Cambridge: Cambridge University Press.
Spaventa, L. (ed.). 1980. *Towards the Creative Teaching of English*. Oxford: Heinemann.

Mêlée games

The following books contain examples of mêlée games similar to those in Chapter 5 which can be used to maintain fluidity and discourage 'cliqueyness' or 'territoriality'.

Hadfield, J. 1984. *Elementary Communication Games*. London: Nelson.
Hadfield, J. 1986. *Intermediate Communication Games*. London: Nelson.
Hadfield, J. 1990. *Advanced Communication Games*. London: Nelson.

Drama and trust activities

The following books are excellent sources of trust and confidence-building activities similar to those in Chapter 7.

Davis, P. and **M. Rinvolucri**. 1990. *The Confidence Book*. London: Longman.
Maley, A. and **A. Duff**. 1980. *Drama Techniques in Language Teaching*. Cambridge: Cambridge University Press.
Wessels, C. 1987. *Drama*. Oxford: Oxford University Press.

Group achievements

The following books are good sources of drama, simulation, or Writing Activities which may be done in groups, similar to the Group Product activities in Chapter 11.

Case, D. and **K. Wilson.** 1979. *Off Stage.* Oxford: Heinemann.
Case, D. and **K. Wilson.** 1984. *Further Off Stage.* Oxford: Heinemann.
Fried-Booth, D. 1986. *Project Work.* Oxford: Oxford University Press.
Geddes, M. and **G. Sturtridge.** 1982. *Video in the Language Classroom.* Oxford: Heinemann.
Hadfield, C. and **J. Hadfield.** 1990. *Writing Games.* London: Nelson.
Jones, K. 1984. *Radio Covingham.* Ismaning, Germany: Max Hueber Verlag.
Jones, L. 1983. *Eight Simulations.* Cambridge: Cambridge University Press.
Maley, A. and **S. Moulding.** 1985. *Poem into Poem.* Cambridge: Cambridge University Press.

A sense of direction

The following book on learner training contains many exercises useful in establishing a sense of direction, setting goals, and choosing appropriate learning strategies, as in Chapters 2 and 16.

Ellis, G. and **B. Sinclair.** 1989. *Learning to Learn English.* Cambridge: Cambridge University Press.

Speaking skills

Some of the techniques described in Chapters 12, 14, and 15 are not activities in their own right, but general techniques that can be used to structure any speaking activity. Activities from the following books may be used in conjunction with the techniques described.

Black, V., M. NcNorton, A. Malderez, and **S. Parker.** 1991. *Speaking: Advanced.* Oxford: Oxford University Press.
Klippel, F. 1985. *Keep Talking.* Cambridge: Cambridge University Press.
Nolasco, R. and **L. Arthur.** 1987. *Conversation.* Oxford: Oxford University Press.
Porter-Ladousse, G. 1983. *Speaking Personally.* Cambridge: Cambridge University Press.
Ur, P. 1981. *Discussions that Work.* Cambridge: Cambridge University Press.
Watcyn-Jones, P. 1981. *Pairwork: A.* London: Penguin.
Watcyn-Jones, P. 1981. *Pairwork: B.* London: Penguin.

Keeping in touch

Examples of authentic English can be found in the following magazines, arranged in order of level from Beginners to Advanced:

Click, Crown, Clockwock, Catch, Club, Current
Available from: MGP Ltd, Brookhampton Lane, Kineton,
    Warwickshire CV35 0JB, UK.

Authentik in English magazine available from: 27 Westland
    Square, Dublin 2, Eire.

For BBC World Service frequencies and times of English-
    language broadcasts, consult:
London Calling, P.O. Box 765, Bush House, The Strand,
    London WC5 4PH, UK.
BBC English Magazine, P.O. Box 96, Cambridge, UK.

Other titles in the Resource Books for Teachers series

Beginners	Peter Grundy
Classroom Dynamics	Jill Hadfield
Conversation	Rob Nolasco and Lois Arthur
Cultural Awareness	Barry Tomalin and Susan Stempleski
Dictionaries	Jonathan Wright
Drama	Charlyn Wessels
Exam Classes	Peter May
Film	Susan Stempleski and Barry Tomalin
Grammar Dictation	Ruth Wajnryb
Homework	Lesley Painter
The Internet	Scott Windeatt, David Hardisty, and David Eastment
Learner-based Teaching	Colin Campbell and Hanna Kryszewska
Letters	Nicky Burbidge, Peta Gray, Sheila Levy, and Mario Rinvolucri
Listening	Goodith White
Literature	Alan Duff and Alan Maley
Music and Song	Tim Murphey
Newspapers	Peter Grundy
Project Work 2nd edition	Diana L. Fried-Booth
Pronunciation	Clement Laroy
Role Play	Gillian Porter Ladousse
Vocabulary	John Morgan and Mario Rinvolucri
Writing	Tricia Hedge

Primary Resource Books

Art and Crafts with Children	Andrew Wright
Assessing Young Learners	Sophie Ioannou-Georgiou and Pavlos Pavlou
Creating Stories with Children	Andrew Wright
Drama with Children	Sarah Phillips
Games for Children	Gordon Lewis with Günther Bedson